SOCCER
SMARTS

SOCCER SMARTS

CHARLIE SLAGLE

75

SKILLS, TACTICS & MENTAL EXERCISES TO IMPROVE YOUR GAME

ROCKRIDGE
PRESS

For general information on our other products and services or to obtain technical sup-port, please contact our Customer Care Department within the United States at (866) 744-2665, or outside the United States at (510) 253-0500.

Rockridge Press publishes its books in a variety of electronic and print formats. Some content that appears in print may not be available in electronic books, and vice versa.

Design: William D. Mack
Editor: Brian Hurley
Production Editor: Erum Khan

Illustrations © Conor Buckley

ISBN: Print 978-1-64152-215-1 | eBook 978-1-64152-216-8

CONTENTS

MENTAL EXERCISES

INTRODUCTION

After more than 30 years as a soccer player, coach, and executive, I've learned that the game is your best teacher. If you want to reach your full potential and become the complete soccer player you were born to be, it would take you a lifetime of constant playing and observing to learn all the aspects of this beautiful game. But most of us are a bit more impatient than that—we want to reach our full potential while we're still alive! That's why I wrote this book: to share what I've learned and help you speed up your lifelong process of becoming a great soccer player.

This book is not for beginners; it is for intermediate and advanced players. Instead of showing you the basic skills, like an inside-of-the-foot pass, I will talk about more advanced skills that rely on those basics.

There are so many ways to teach soccer skills and tactics, and so many ways for a coach to handle the various 11 v 11 matchups. I have decided to break the game down to its three major components: physical skills that you can sharpen as an individual player, clever tactics to use with your teammates, and mental exercises to improve your understanding of the game itself.

We'll start by taking a close look at your physical skills. You should always measure yourself against your own physical potential—not against your teammates or the superstars you see on TV. Proper strength and conditioning will expand your knowledge of the game and help make you the best type of player you can be. A coach like me can help you with this, but you need to take personal responsibility for your training and conditioning in order to meet the physical demands of the game.

Next, we'll talk about many of the tactics you can use on the field with your teammates. When should you try to dribble by the opponent? Where you should run when your teammate is about to cross the ball, and how quickly should you get to your final destination? How should you help your teammate defend? How should you help your teammate with the ball at their feet? Your physical skills will enable you to play well, but you need to be familiar with these tactics to know how to apply those skills.

Finally, if you want to be a complete player, you need to understand the game as a whole. What can you do to increase your team's chances to score when you have a 20-yard free kick? How can you defend against your opponents in the middle of the field to limit their chances of going forward? As a player, understanding the game and being able to transfer that knowledge on the pitch makes you a valuable member of the team. I'll show you how to take advantage of your soccer knowledge to make your team better.

If you are a goalkeeper, there are plenty of chapters that specifically address your position. As a former goalkeeper myself (once a goalkeeper, always a goalkeeper!), I think it would behoove you to read every single chapter. The goalkeepers are the only players who can see all the other players on the field at all times. Knowing what they are doing will improve your goalkeeping and enable you to speak up and help your team defensively and offensively. Goalkeepers need to be leaders; it is the nature of the position. Knowing the game inside and out will help you be that leader.

You can read this book straight through, or you can skip around to find a skill you want to work on. You'll see a difficulty level for each skill marked on the edge of the page—use those to work your way up to the more challenging ones. Each skill comes with a tip at the end to push your knowledge a little further. And, just for fun, I included some of my favorite quotes from world-class soccer players.

I hope you enjoy this book. I hope you will find plenty of encouragement and insights. Like I said, the game is your best teacher. Make an effort to learn every time you are on the field or watching others play, and you will be heading in the right direction.

SKILLS

It may seem obvious, but it's worth mentioning— soccer starts with your body. It's about how you move, how you respond, how you find room to be creative. These are your core skills, and the only way to acquire them is by practicing them. In this section, I'll cover the basic skills that can make you a better soccer player. Some are simple, some are complex, but all of them can be practiced and perfected. There's no such thing as too much of any particular skill.

1

1 v 1 Defending:
Don't Get Beat Behind

Defending

Defending is arguably the most important part of the game. After all, if you can keep the other team from scoring, you can't lose—at worst, you'll draw. With a bit of luck and some skilled offense, you might even win.

The object of defending is to not get beat behind—either off the dribble or a combination of passes. Whether you're a back, a midfielder, or a striker, defending requires a compact stance—one I like to call the broken-down position. In this position, the knees are bent, you are on the balls of your feet with one foot in front of the other, and your focus is on both your opponent and the ball. Some refer to the broken-down position as "getting small"—a much harder position to beat than the "tall," upright position you assume when running between marks. When your opponent makes a dribbling move, you're a lot easier to beat if you're standing upright *(see Figure 1.1)*.

Figure 1.1

When defending, the distance you keep from your opponent depends on their speed and offensive skill. The better and/or faster a player is, the more room you need to give them. Good defending forces the offensive player to look down at the ball and limits their options.

Regardless of position, every player on the field has a role to play in defending. And team defending starts with 1 versus 1 (1 v 1) defending.

Practicing 1 v 1 defense with a teammate can be as simple as playing 1 v 1 and trying to not get beat behind. If you're on your own, you might practice getting into the broken-down position and moving in different directions while being light on your feet. Remember: The object is to keep your opponent from getting past you. When that happens, your teammates have to cover for you, leaving more time and space for your opponent with the ball to make potentially damaging plays (not a good thing).

Don't try to force a steal. Stealing the ball happens when your opponent makes a mistake, giving you a clear opportunity to steal it. As a defender, "diving" in with a foot leaves you vulnerable to getting beat.

SKILL

2

Dribbling Moves:
Finish Your Defender

Dribbling

The goal of 1 v 1 offense is, quite simply, to get past your opponent and keep them behind you. If you want defenders perpetually eating your dust, you need to master a few dribbling moves—moves that you can use consistently (and successfully) in competition. Let's break down the most basic anatomy of a good dribbling move *(see Figure 1.2)*.

First, if you really want to beat a defender, it's best to take them on at speed when possible. In other words, you want to come at the defender at a rapid pace while maintaining control of the ball. Taking on the defender at speed can leave them on their heels rather than in a good, broken-down defensive stance.

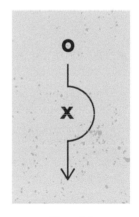

Figure 1.2

Once you have a defender on their heels, make a move to push them further off-balance. This might take the form of stepping over the ball and then pushing it to the side, or chopping the ball using the inside or outside of the foot.

With your defender fully off-balance, it's time to apply the beating touch—essentially moving the ball past them. To truly beat your defender, the beating touch must be dynamic and done at a speed.

Unfortunately, many players are content with stopping after the beating touch, but letting up once you're just past a defender gives them (or another defensive player) an opportunity to stifle your forward movement. It's a bit like throwing your hands up in victory as soon as you pull ahead in a track race—but before everyone has crossed the finish line. Sure, you're ahead in that moment, but you haven't really won yet. To cement your position ahead of your opponent, you need a finishing touch—one where you get behind the defender and the only options they have are to follow you or foul you. Either way, your defender is now in a position they're trying to avoid at all costs.

Focus on two to four "go-to" dribbling moves. Too many times, players try to take on too many moves. You'll be a lot more successful at beating your opponent with two to four perfected moves than with a whole catalog of so-so ones. When practicing dribbling moves, challenge yourself to go as fast as you can. Sure, you might fall down by stepping on the ball, but once you've mastered moves at speed, they will pay dividends on the field.

Keep the Ball: Use Your Body

Dribbling

When you have the ball, it's best to try to keep it that way. One of the most important skills you can master is shielding: making it as hard as possible for your opponent to get the ball by using your body to protect it. You want to use your body to keep your opponent as far away from the ball as possible.

When shielding, make your body as "wide" as possible. To do this, face sideways with the ball at your foot away from your defender. Your feet should be apart, and you should keep your opponent on your back shoulder to create as much distance as possible. To make even more distance, play the ball with the outside of your lead foot.

Whenever you're in possession of the ball, it's good to know where your opponent is. This way, you know when your defender is trying to make a move to win the ball. To get an easy read on your opponent's whereabouts, make body contact. Since your body stance should already be wide, the defender should not be able to poke the ball away without choosing a side. If they go to your right to try to win the ball, you go left. If they go left, you go right. Making physical contact frees up both time and space—giving you more opportunities to beat your defender on the dribble or find a teammate with a pass.

In the same realm, you can also use your body to do a spin turn. Picture this scenario: You are dribbling toward the touchline and a defender is right on you. You have no passing options and you're running out of room. As you get close to the touch, you take a long step with the foot nearest your defender to shield the ball. You then stop and play the ball with the outside of the opposite foot, turning back and facing forward on the field, giving you time and space for other options.

Joe Cole, the former English international player who has continued his career in the United States, is especially adept at the spin turn anywhere on the field. Upper- and lower-body strength are essential for shielding and spin turns. Work on these physical aspects to become a better player.

Dynamic Step Overs

Dribbling

One of the most effective dribbling moves is the step over, which is essentially what it sounds like and can be done at any speed, over a moving or stationary ball. The step over can throw a defender off-balance by creating the illusion that you are going to make a move around the defender or pass the ball to a teammate. It gives you time to either beat the defender on the dribble or pass to a teammate.

To learn the step over, start with a stationary ball. Standing behind the ball, move your right foot to left side of the ball (your right foot will pass between the ball and your left foot), continuing the movement around the rest of the ball. To do the step over with your left foot, begin by bringing your left foot to the right side of the ball and go around it. Start slowly and work on your balance. To help with your balance, use your arms, which will help keep you stable and allow for dynamic movement.

Once you've mastered the step over with a stationary ball, try it on a moving ball. As you get more adept, speed up the pace of the ball as well as the time it takes to do the step over. The next step is to do multiple step overs by pushing the ball in front of you and doing as many step overs in a row as you can. Lastly, work on alternating step overs from one foot to the other, doing multiple step overs on the moving ball.

> It is important that your movement around the ball is done dynamically. Watch players at the top level do the step over. You might see a player like Lionel Messi unbalance a player on a stationary ball. Because he has such great control of the ball, many defenders will be reluctant to reach in and commit for the ball for fear that he will beat them. Watch the best and emulate them.

I DON'T BELIEVE SKILL WAS, OR EVER WILL BE, THE RESULT OF COACHES. IT IS A RESULT OF A LOVE AFFAIR BETWEEN THE CHILD AND THE BALL.

—ROY MAURICE KEANE

5

Receive the Ball to Play It

Receiving

I once heard a coach talk about receiving or "trapping" the ball like trapping a bird in a box. To trap a bird, you sprinkle some birdseed on the ground and prop up a box with a stick attached to a string. When the bird goes after the seed, you pull the string and trap the bird. But what happens next? You need to have a plan. The same is true of trapping a ball and stopping it underneath you. You need to know what comes next.

You can't be satisfied with simply stopping the ball. You need to receive the ball in a way that allows you to do something with it—whether that's passing or immediately taking off on a dribble. If a ball is on the ground, you should be able to use all parts of your foot to go anywhere in a 360-degree area around you. You must control the pace of the ball so that it doesn't go too far away from you, allowing it to be stolen. You also don't want to receive the ball too close to your body, forcing you to either back up to play it or make an extra "setup" touch to play it.

The same is true if you receive the ball with your chest: You need to receive it and direct the ball to a place where you can play your next touch safely. Receiving with the chest limits you to fewer than 360 degrees of direction change, but the more directions that you can receive to play, the better.

> As your receiving skills improve, try practicing with a defender. This way, you'll gain experience deciding where to direct the ball when receiving it, depending on the defender's position.

NEVER ASSUME GREATNESS IS FOR SOMEONE ELSE. IMAGINE EVERY DAY THAT YOU TOO CAN DO GREAT THINGS. HAVE THE COURAGE TO TAKE THE CHALLENGE, MAKE THE MISTAKES, AND MOVE FORWARD.

—BRANDI CHASTAIN

Juggling: Be Creative and Test Yourself

Possession

You can greatly improve your ball-control skills by juggling—and all you need to practice is a ball and some space. Juggling on the thighs is easiest simply because they are a bigger surface to bounce the ball on than the feet, head, and other parts of the body. To get the most out of your juggling exercises, put some parameters on them. While juggling with your feet, make it more challenging by pointing your toes when contacting the ball like you do when you shoot. You can also sit on the ground with your legs outstretched and try to juggle with your feet. This kind of juggling will help your control on the field.

Another juggling exercise is to try and go "around the world." In around the world, start juggling with one foot, advance to the thigh, and then to the shoulder (if you start with the right foot, you use the right thigh and right shoulder or vice versa if you start with the left foot), then your head to the opposite shoulder, thigh, and foot. Then, try to go back again in the opposite direction. If you find yourself struggling with this exercise, first try breaking it down into components, like trying to do shoulder to head to opposite shoulder, before putting all the pieces together.

Another juggling exercise is to make every fourth (or some other number) juggle go at least double your height and then continue juggling. You can also juggle by popping the ball over your head, forcing yourself to turn around with the ball in midair to keep juggling. Juggling on the move adds more skill to your workout. See how fast or how far you can go.

Challenge yourself by trying new and more difficult things when juggling. Don't get in a rut and do the same thing over and over. Players get better when they have difficulty doing something at first but, with practice, master it.

Group Juggling

Possession

Juggling is a great way to develop touch on the ball. When you juggle by yourself, you get plenty of touches, but you always know where the ball is coming from because you were the last one to touch it. Group juggling exercises bring a factor of the unknown into play, since a friend or teammate may put the ball somewhere you are not expecting.

One of the group juggling scenarios I like most is to have a set number of touches that each player has to play the ball. For example, you may have a mandatory two touches every time you get the ball. You can also play a progression juggling drill where the first player gets one touch, the second gets two touches, the third three touches, and the fourth player four. After the fourth player does four touches, the next player begins again with one touch. In both of these, the group tries to get as many touches as possible without letting the ball hit the ground.

Another exercise is to play "No Thighs"—something like the juggling equivalent of "Horse" in basketball. The goal is to be the last player standing. To play, players juggle the ball together. If you lose the ball or the ball hits your thigh, you get a letter. When a player gets eight letters (No Thighs), they are out. This little game can get very competitive. If there is disagreement over who gets a letter when the ball hits the ground, the decision goes to the crowd.

Another fun juggling game is Soccer Tennis, which you can play with a net or cones. The object is to put the ball over the net (or the line between the cones) and not let it drop on your side or out of bounds. You can make your own rules as to how many touches a player can use. Usually, only three individuals can play the ball on their side of the net before clearing the net (like volleyball). You might play to 11 points or whatever you decide.

In all juggling exercises, try to play every ball, no matter how far away it is. You don't get perfect balls every time during games, so the movement and contortion of your body is good practice.

8

Power Shooting: Hammer It

Shooting

To get better at striking the ball hard and accurately, you have to, well, practice striking the ball as hard as you can. Obviously, hitting the ball hard enhances your chance of scoring; a faster moving ball means the goalkeeper has less time to react. Of course, to score, the ball must be on goal and accurate, but we will get to that later.

To strike the ball hard, use the instep of your foot. In other words, hit the ball with the laces of your shoe. To make your shooting surface firm, your toe should be down and your ankle locked. Both the swing of your leg and your last stride into the ball are very important for giving you maximum power. If possible, make a long stride with your plant foot—a move that will get more of your body weight into the kick. Be careful not to get to the ball too quickly. I call this getting "foot-tied." It keeps you from taking a long stride, throws off the rhythm of the kick, and takes away a great deal of power.

As you work on hammering it, practice with dead balls, moving balls from your dribbling, rolling balls that are coming toward you, and volleys. With the volleys, toss the ball into the air and hit it close to the ground just before it bounces or, to make it easier, just before the second bounce.

Once you can strike the ball hard, it's time to worry about hitting it accurately. To start, make sure you are hitting the center of the ball. Not only will this help you stay accurate, but it will also make sure the ball doesn't spin and take any speed away from your kick. Also, know where you are going to kick the ball (the near post, the far post, etc.). Be insightful and make small changes—ones that allow you to put the ball where you want it to go without losing any power.

All coaches like players that can strike a ball hard and accurately. Conversely, most opposing coaches and goalkeepers do not like opponents that can strike it well. It is well worth the time investment it takes to kick the ball hard and straight.

Volleys: Don't Be Satisfied Just Hitting It

Shooting

Hitting the ball out of the air is called a volley. This makes it easier to make a ball dip, which increases your chance of scoring on the shot. Why? Because the ball could go over the goalkeeper at a height higher than the goal (eight feet), then dip down behind them to score. To make a ball dip, follow through with the knee of your shooting leg going in an upward motion. This puts topspin on the ball, making it dip.

Volleys can also yield a swerving ball that can be hit with either the inside or the outside of the shooting foot. To achieve this swerving effect, hit the ball in the center and follow through to the side of the ball. If using the outside of the right foot, follow through to the left; for the inside of the right foot, follow through to the right. This causes sidespin, making the ball curl. As with dipping, this allows the shooter to aim outside of the goalpost and potentially swerve around the goalkeeper, making it much more difficult to defend against. Of course, volleying isn't just about adding spin. With a volley, it is also easier to hit the ball dead center, causing the ball to have no spin at all. This causes a knuckleball effect, making the ball move erratically and making it more difficult for the goalkeeper to save. Of course, like a knuckleball in baseball, this takes a lot of practice to perfect. As you work on it, pay attention to what works and try to replicate the same kind of contact to repeatedly hit knuckleballs.

Volleying can be a very productive skill. As a goalkeeper, I was more worried about facing a volley because they're so unpredictable; the ball could dip, knuckle, or curl. Of course, it is not as easy to hit a volley as it is to hit a ball on the ground, but becoming proficient at hitting volleys will make you a better player.

10

Long Balls: Get Elevation

Passing

During a game, you sometimes need to kick a long ball to clear a ball down the field when the opposition is pressuring your team, during free kicks and goal kicks from dead balls, or when hitting crosses from a moving ball. Proper technique—and a lot of practice—can make you better at hitting long balls as needed.

A long free kick requires the ability to kick the ball firmly, get the ball in the air, make the ball travel a long distance, and have the ball go where you want it to go. To kick the ball firmly, hit the center of the ball from side to side; otherwise it will spin and not go as far as it could. Getting the ball in the air requires you to hit from a slightly acute angle and strike the ball with your instep, just off-center from your laces. To really get the ball in the air, lean back and hit it below the midpoint. The lower you go from the midpoint, the higher the ball will go. Experiment to see where you need to hit the ball to make it achieve your desired height. Lastly, follow through, with your kicking leg going up toward the sky.

In kicking crosses, much of the technique is unchanged; you are just kicking the ball across your body. To do this well, in your last stride to the ball, open your body by taking a step toward the target with your plant foot and pointing that foot toward the target.

Just like in power shooting, it is important to take a long last stride into a long ball. Doing this puts your body weight through the ball, thus increasing the power.

I WORKED ON MY WEAKNESSES
AND MADE THEM MY STRENGTHS.

—SYDNEY LEROUX

Heading & Throw-Ins: Put Your Back Into It

Heading

You might be surprised to see heading and throw-ins combined here. However, one of the power sources used to head the ball is the same as the source for throwing the ball in for distance: arching the back and snapping your body forward.

For throw-ins, timing is at least as important as power. For the strongest throw, release the ball in conjunction with your upper body snapping forward. Practice this by starting on your knees, arching your back and snapping forward, and throwing the ball in compliance with the rules. Once you've mastered the throw-in from your knees, practice standing up like you will in a match.

Many times, you'll see a player running up to the touchline to provide power for a long throw-in. While this is more difficult than snapping your body forward on the throw, it can lengthen the distance of your throw when combined with the snapping of the back.

While using your back means one thing, using your head has a dual meaning. Of course, coaches want their players to play intelligently. However, your head is also a surface that can play the ball. Heading can be used to shoot the ball, pass the ball, and clear the ball, and proper technique is very important. Done poorly, heading can lead to injuries like concussions. To head the ball, use your forehead—and make sure that you strike the ball rather than letting the ball strike you.

When heading, power comes from forward movement—movement you can achieve by using your neck to propel your head forward. You can move your head forward in a more powerful motion by arching your back and then dynamically thrusting your upper body forward, as you do when throwing in. This motion, combined with the head snapping forward from the neck and striking the ball properly with your forehead, will produce the maximum heading power. When heading balls above your head, jump straight up and, at the apex of your jump, snap your head forward using your back and neck.

To increase your throw even further, work on the flexibility and strength of your back. Gymnasts who play soccer can usually throw the ball exceedingly far because of their immense back strength and flexibility.

12

One-Touch Passing: Keep the Ball

Passing

When receiving the ball, you always need to have a one-touch passing option available. Why? Because when the defense closes in, getting rid of the ball quickly and successfully can mean the difference between keeping the ball and losing it.

When making a pass with the inside of your foot, your plant foot needs to face your target, and the toe of your playing foot needs to be pointed up to ensure your ankle is locked. This allows you to make a firmer and more accurate pass. If the ankle is not locked and the foot is floppy, you can't hit as hard and your accuracy diminishes. To keep the ball from popping up and to provide topspin so that the ball rolls smoothly, strike the ball just above the center.

To practice, use a kick wall or some other flat surface that you won't damage. Be light on your feet, and see how many firm passes you can make consecutively. With a partner, you can pass back and forth using one-touch passing. Try to keep the ball on the ground. Errors will occur once the ball starts bouncing or comes back in the air. Add a third or fourth player to practice making passes to the right and left, as well as right back where it came from. In these groups, make the distance from player to player longer to practice distance one-touch passing. Finally, add some movement to your practice.

The best players and teams are able to use accurate one-touch passing to maintain ball possession. Ultimately, you want to hit the ball near the ankle with your foot square to the ball. This allows for a bigger surface area and will give you more margin of error in making a good pass.

WHEN PEOPLE SUCCEED, IT IS BECAUSE OF HARD WORK. LUCK HAS NOTHING TO DO WITH SUCCESS.

—DIEGO MARADONA

Goalkeeper Shot Blocking

Goalkeeping

As a goalkeeper, your main duty is to keep balls out of the net. In other words, you need to be able to block shots. Beyond stopping the ball, it is also hugely important that you don't allow rebounds.

Catching the ball is a sure way to eliminate any rebound. First, position your body in the ball's direct path so that if it goes through your hands, your body will be there to block it. Catch the ball equally with both hands, making sure that your fingers engulf the ball. Make sure that the ends of your fingers are at the top. If a ball goes through your hands on a higher ball (say, one over your head), your body won't be there to stop it. As the shot comes into your hands, allowing your hands to gently give will help you to catch the ball. Having "soft hands" is a huge asset for any goalkeeper.

When you face a longer shot and you have opponents around you, you need to catch the ball if at all possible. When facing a shot with great velocity, you can, using soft hands, let the ball drop in front of you and then pick it up. This technique may be a safer option than trying to catch a blazing shot or a ball that is knuckling.

When diving for a ball, the catching technique is similar. You want your hands to engulf the ball. Of course, catching is imperative on a diving save (because you will be on the ground, and if you don't catch the ball, you will give up a rebound). If you dive for a shot and can't catch the ball, parry it to safety, which usually results in a corner kick. To parry the ball, use your hands to direct the ball outside of the goalpost. It is much better to allow a corner kick in this situation than to allow a goal or a rebound.

> As a goalkeeper, you can never practice blocking shots too often. However, at no time should you face shots casually or, for that matter, when tired. Get your fitness outside of shot blocking and train shot blocking while fresh.

Goalkeeping: Facing High Balls

Goalkeeping

When a ball is in the air from a cross or a corner kick, it is important that the goalkeeper catches it or puts it out of danger. When catching the ball, you need to be in a position where you can jump straight up in the air to make the catch. Jump straight up and catch the ball at the highest point for your jumping ability. You should train to get as high as you can by using your legs and arms to maximize your vertical leap. To protect yourself from opponents, when you jump off your left foot, hitch your right leg into the air, and keep that leg up with your thigh parallel to the ground. At your apex and with great timing, gather the ball in with a solid catch. When coming down to the ground, goalkeepers often make a mistake by bringing the ball to their chest. You should keep your arms stretched above you as you come down. Bringing the ball down earlier makes too many moving parts. With the ball above your head as you land, the referee will protect you if you get bumped by an opponent.

If you can't catch a high ball due to traffic in the box or your misjudgment, the safe technique is to punch or "box" the ball. When punching the ball, use your arm to create the boxing motion. Punch by using your elbow to propel your fist. A common mistake is to use your wrist, which is risky and can lead to injury. When punching the ball, hit it hard and high out of danger.

Lastly, if you can't catch or punch the ball, parry it using your palm and fingers to guide the ball to safety. If you do parry it, quickly get back into position. You may need to face a shot from the rebound caused by the parry.

When facing high balls, your form is as important as timing. Make sure that you train with opposition in the penalty area. It's important to practice avoiding obstacles, simulating a game situation.

15

Hitch Kick/Bicycle: Expand Your Shooting Range

Shooting

When a ball is high off the ground and you want to hit a first-time shot, you need to perfect the hitch kick. If the ball is knee height or higher, due to pesky anatomy, you can't volley the ball effectively. Don't believe me? Try it, and watch as your foot gets under the ball and the ball soars over the goal. The hitch kick can allow you to make solid contact and hit a high-quality shot when a ball is in a tougher position.

So what can you do? You can elevate your body to allow for a controlled volley. To do this, jump up off your soon-to-be shooting foot. With the opposite leg, forcefully bring your nonshooting leg upward, bringing you higher off the ground. Now, with the ball high off the ground, strike it like a volley.

The hitch-kicking motion is also used in one of the most exciting skills in soccer: the bicycle kick. With the ball overhead, a player jumps off their soon-to-be shooting foot and then hitch kicks the other leg. Then, with body parallel to the ground, the player hits the ball like a volley. A bicycle kick will cause you to land on your back, so be prepared to cushion the fall with your hands. As with a volley, goalkeepers do not like facing a bicycle kick, because they don't know

Figure 1.3

where it is going *(see Figure 1.3)*. Honestly, most of the time, the kicker doesn't see either.

Practicing a bicycle kick can be painful due to landing on your back. To practice in a less painful way, use a high-jump/pole-vault pit. An even more fun (and cool) way to practice is to go to a decently shallow spot in a lake or pool, and let the water break your fall. If practicing in the water, you may want to use a beach ball.

> Remember: Soccer is a contact sport (don't let anyone tell you that it isn't). You must be able to play effectively when knocked off-balance. Practicing skills where you have to put your body in different positions, such as the hitch kick and bicycle, helps you in game situations.

Side Volleys: Strike Them Down

Shooting

Picture a ball to your right side in the penalty area, about waist high. Many times, players will trap this ball and take one or more touches to bring it under control. The time that it takes to do this allows the goalkeeper and teammates to prepare for your next play, thus making it difficult to score. However, using a powerful side volley will give you a good chance of burying the ball in the back of the net.

To strike a side volley when you are facing the ball, turn your plant foot (your left foot in this case) to face the goal and spin your body, raising your shooting foot parallel to the ground and strike the ball—all in one motion. Use your arms to enhance your body spin and provide balance. Your power is generated in two ways: the kicking motion and the dynamic turn of your body. Your shooting foot should have the toe pointed down to provide a strong strike.

A flying side volley is a skill that joins the ranks of a bicycle kick and other "exotic" skills. Like the bicycle kick, the flying side volley will be used when striking a ball above your waist. To complete a flying side volley, follow the same steps as the standard side volley, all while jumping upward. Sound hard? Well, it is—and it requires practice. As with a bicycle kick, the flying side volley means landing with your body on the ground. To help eliminate pain when practicing, use a mat to land on or practice in the shallow end of a pool or lake.

When practicing side volleys, try to strike the ball at an angle to hit the goal line on a shot. You can do this by hitting the ball a little bit above its center. This way, even a slight miss still has a chance to score. It's always better to kick low than high.

TO WATCH PEOPLE PUSH THEMSELVES FURTHER THAN THEY THINK THEY CAN, IT'S A BEAUTIFUL THING.

—ABBY WAMBACH

TACTICS

Individual players don't win soccer games; teams do. So if you want to win, you need to be the best teammate possible. That means working with your teammates at an almost subconscious level to set up an attack, swarm your opponents, or connect for an unbelievable assist. In this section we'll look at the ways you can improve your game by working effectively with your teammates.

Receiving the Ball:
Give Yourself Options

Possession

Many times in a game, you hear a player say, "Pass me the ball, I'm open." However, in reality, that player might not be open. The player with the ball needs a clear path to pass before anyone is really "open" *(see Figure 2.1)*.

The first step to getting open is to get into an open passing lane. Even so, you might be in an open passing lane but still marked very tightly. If this is the case, check away from the ball and check to the open passing lane. An effective check away and check back can allow you more space to receive the ball. Also, when you are picking a position to receive the ball, make sure you have options to pass it either with one or two touches.

Once you're truly open, you can ask for the ball verbally, or you can physically show your teammate you are open by being in a good receiving position. This might mean being a big target with your hands out for balance and looking ready to get

the ball. In the long run, your
success in your pass to a
teammate after receiving the
ball will determine whether
you get passed to again. Make
good passes that retain possession or spring someone to goal,
and the ball will come to you
again and again. If you lose the
ball at your feet or make passes

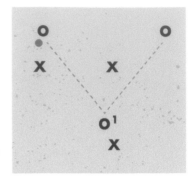

Figure 2.1

that lose possession, you'll find that your teammates won't pass
to you very often—and the coach may not play you as much.

> Watch a lot of soccer. Focus on how players get
> open to receive a pass and into position to pass to
> a teammate. With every pass by your team, adjust your
> positioning to be open for a pass.

2

Play the Way You Face

Possession

When your team has possession of the ball, the fewer touches you use, the more likely you will be to maintain it. You will hear many coaches tell their teams to play the way you face. It is easier to play the way you are facing because you can easily make one-touch passes and you can see all your available options. Not only does turning to play the ball require more than one touch, but you will also need to visually find your teammates after you turn to deliver the pass. Also, your closest opponent might be behind you, meaning you could be pressured or tackled before you can get the pass off.

As you open yourself up for a pass, survey the area around you to see the best passing options. If the best option is to the right, then adjust your body to be facing the right when you receive the ball. You will not be receiving the ball the way you face, but you will be passing the ball the way you face.

As a team, help your teammates receiving the ball know their options. If the receiving player is unmarked, let them know to turn the ball. If a defender is bearing down on the player receiving the ball, say "man on," alerting your teammate not to turn and play the way the teammate is facing. Be the eyes in the back of your teammate's head. This way, your teammate has the information necessary to make good choices playing the ball.

A talking team is usually a better team—but that's only true if the talking team is relaying information that can benefit the team as a whole. As a team, remember: You must play for one another.

IN FOOTBALL, THE WORST BLINDNESS
IS ONLY SEEING THE BALL.
—NELSON FALCÃO RODRIGUES

Get Open: Make Runs

Possession

So you want to get open for a pass to come to you, or open up space for another teammate to be open. One great strategy is to make as many blind-sided runs as possible. What is a blind-sided run? It is a run where the player guarding you cannot see you and the ball at the same time. Your defender must make a choice as to whether to see the ball, you, or a combination of the ball and you by turning their head. None of these choices are a positive for the defender. If the defender loses track of the ball, they may keep up with you but won't know when a pass may be coming. If the defender watches the ball, then they won't know where you are to receive the ball. You do not want to make too many runs in front of the defender. When you do, they can see you and the ball and can read the play, allowing them to be more effective on defense *(see Figure 2.2)*.

In team defense, defenders like to have support from a teammate. If a defender has support, they can channel the player with the ball toward the supporting player, all the while getting closer to their mark with the ball. If your defender is in a good position to help a defender on the ball, make a run that takes your defender away from a support position. You can do this by running away from the ball. If your defender follows you, the support is gone; if your defender stays in support, then you are open. You can also run around your teammate with the ball, making your defender leave

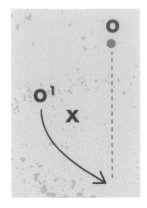

Figure 2.2

their supporting position. That overlapping move can free you up—plus, your teammate with the ball might now be free to make a dribbling move to beat their defender.

A run in front of your defender can be effective if you are trying to open space for another teammate who runs into the space you just vacated. Your defender will watch you and the ball and would have a difficult time supporting a teammate who is guarding your teammate running into the open space.

4

Runs for Crosses: Get Open and Finish

Scoring

When your team is crossing the ball, it is important to make great runs during the run of play on a corner kick or free kick on the flank. Hopefully, you will have multiple teammates making runs. If three runners are available, one should go to a near-post position, one in the middle, and one on the far post.

If you are making the near-post run, get just in front of the near post, about four to six yards from the end line. If the ball comes to you, redirect it toward the goal or dummy the ball. The dummy can be effective since it forces the opposing goalkeeper to respect your ability to redirect the ball, meaning they have to cover the near post. If you dummy the ball, the goalkeeper is out of position to cover the back post when your teammate plays the ball. If you make the near-post run and the ball is unplayable, turn to the goal and get in position for any ball coming back your way *(see Figure 2.3)*.

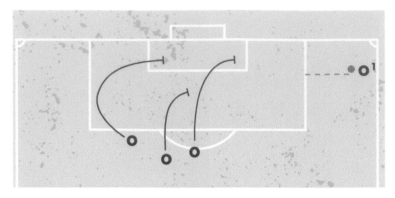

Figure 2.3

If you are the middle runner, you should get around the penalty spot and survey the play. See where the cross is flighted and get to a position to play the ball. After surveying possible cross outcomes, make a dynamic move where you can play the ball.

If you are running to the back post, time your run so that you arrive as the ball does. This makes you harder to guard. If there is a defender in your ideal spot, try to get in front of them as the cross arrives. This will give you a better chance to score. Don't just stand there waiting for the ball, as you become an easy mark for a defender. If the ball does come to you and the goal is open on your near post, place the ball there. If not, a good move is to play the ball back to your far post. There, it can be played by your teammates that made the other runs if saved or just wide.

The teammate that is the farthest back should direct the other players verbally. If you are that farthest back player, you can see the other players and direct them to positions of near post, far post, and middle. These verbal decisions will provide dividends for your team in the form of goals.

Crosses: Set the Table

Scoring

When crossing the ball, you must first and foremost take the goalkeeper out of the play. Since they can use their hands, goalkeepers have an advantage on any ball in the air. A ball right in front of the goal might work in youth competitions, where goalkeepers are not as adept. With more experienced goalkeepers, balls directly in front of their net are easy pickings. Therefore, on a lofted cross, keep the ball away from the goalkeeper. In a game, you must determine from previous plays how big of a range the goalkeeper has and keep the ball out of the goalkeeper's comfort zone *(see Figure 2.4)*.

A crosser has three general aiming points for balls in the air. The first is the near-post ball. This ball is a driven ball about two to six yards off the end line where a teammate can redirect it on goal. The second aiming point is in the middle of the goal about eight to 12 yards out—a distance determined by the goalkeeper's range. The last aiming point is a more lofted back-post ball. This ball should be, once again, outside the

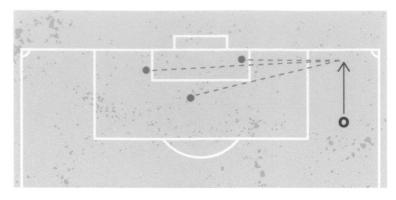

Figure 2.4

goalkeeper's range and ideally four to 10 yards off the goal line.
This gives a great opportunity for a teammate to make a run to
the far post and strike the ball hard toward the net. When
playing these crosses to the center or the back post, it is good
to curl the ball with the inside of the foot. This will increase the
odds of your teammate getting a good shot.

Crossers can also hit a driven ball to the near post on the
ground. This is only effective if at least one of your teammates
is making a near-post run. The ball needs to be hit at great
speed so that your front-post teammate can dummy the ball or
redirect it in front of the net. On crosses, the more confusion in
front of the net, the better for the offense.

Even though an early cross (18-plus yards from the
end line) can be effective, it is a good tactic to carry
the ball nearer to the end line to cross. The angle from nearer
the end line is better for your teammates to finish, and it greatly
lessens the chance of a teammate being caught offside.

TACTIC

6

2 v 1 Overlapping: Spread the Defense

Possession

When your teammate has the ball and you make a run from behind to the outside of your teammate, it's called overlapping. An overlapping run unbalances the other team's defense by making the defender guarding your teammate with the ball worry about you. That defender now has to make a decision to stop the dribbler or not allow you to get the ball at speed on the outside. This confusion and decision-making by the defender makes your team more dangerous *(see Figure 2.5)*.

To make the overlap effective, a few things need to happen. First, the overlapper must go behind your teammate with the ball. If you run in front of your teammate, the first defender can step up and press the ball hard when you are in a position directly behind the defender. If you run behind your teammate, then you are in a position to receive a safe pass if the defender steps up hard. You must also make your run dynamic. A

47

jogging overlap is usually an
unsuccessful overlap. Make your
overlap with a purpose.

Also, let your teammate know
you are overlapping. Since you can
see the whole play, your teammate
needs to know there is help
coming. Verbally letting your
teammate know that you are
overlapping puts the defender on

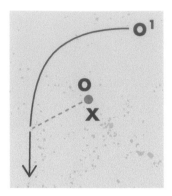

Figure 2.5

notice. Soon after knowing that you are overlapping, it is your
teammate's responsibility to make room for your run by
dribbling at the defender at speed and to the inside. This will
give your teammate two options: to pass to you streaking down
the outside or to try to beat a conflicted opponent 1 v 1.

It is imperative to remember that any 2 v 1 offensive
situation is made better by keeping the 1 v 1 as part
of the 2 v 1. The player with the ball must always keep the
1 v 1 move in play. In fact, the 1 v 1 move is enhanced by
a 2 v 1 move.

What to Do When You Have the Ball

Possession

The question of what to do when you have the ball is not always a simple one—and it begins before you have the ball. Before you can begin to answer it, you need to read the landscape of the field to see where there are positive options for playing the ball quickly. You need to assess the defense. If one player is an excellent defender and is in good position to defend, you may want to find a teammate to pass to quickly to keep possession. If that defender isn't quite as good or will be late to pressure the ball, you may want to attack that player off the dribble. If your defender is coming at you at a high rate of speed and hasn't broken down defensively, you might want to one touch the ball by the defender and beat them up the field.

If your marker isn't as fast as you, consider taking the ball down the flank where the defender has less help. You might even see whether you can play a dangerous cross into the penalty area. There are many scenarios—and your scenarios may be different from a teammate's options when receiving the ball. It depends on your skill with the ball at your feet, the part of the field that you are located at that time, the quality of the player marking you, and your team's style of play.

Your position on the field is a big factor when receiving the ball. The farther forward on the field that you are, the more chances you can take. (If you lose the ball, you have many teammates behind you to stop a counterattack.) Playing in your final third, you can take chances to try to beat your defender and break down the defense. In the midfield or center third of the field, you can take some chances offensively, but not as many as in the final third. In the middle third, you might only have the backs behind you to thwart a counterattack. In your defensive third, you do not want to take any chances, because a lost ball could lead to a great opportunity for your opponent.

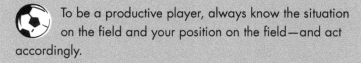
To be a productive player, always know the situation on the field and your position on the field—and act accordingly.

Pressuring the Ball Defensively: Be Solid

Defense

Pressuring the ball both as an individual and as a collective unit can make your squad a much better team. Defending is about not getting beat behind. When you get beat, all of your teammates must adjust their positions—many times leaving openings that your opponent can make into an offensive advantage. Remember: If you play defense only to win the ball, you give the other team an opportunity when you miss. The more opportunities the opposition has, the better their chances of scoring.

When you are with an opponent in a 1 v 1 situation and you have little to no help, the word "delay" should be ringing in your ears. Get into a position where your opponent cannot make a penetrating pass. That same position must stop your mark from dribbling past you. In this way, you're delaying the opponent's attack and allowing your teammates time to get back into a good defensive position. If an opponent has time with the ball and no pressure, that opponent will be able to wait until a teammate gets open on a run, thus breaking down the defense.

> Practice makes perfect. Play 1 v 1 over and over and over again. 1 v 1 is the foundation of the game of soccer. Practice both sides of the ball and get good at both. Doing so will make you a well-rounded player.

TRUE CHAMPIONS AREN'T ALWAYS THE ONES THAT WIN, BUT THOSE WITH THE MOST GUTS.

—MIA HAMM

TACTIC 9

Give-and-Go: One-Two to Break Down the Defense

Combination Play

A very effective (and the most common) 2 v 1 combination play is the give-and-go. The player with the ball attacks their defender at speed with the ball as in a 1 v 1 situation. A teammate of the dribbler then opens up for a pass and receives one. The teammate then returns a pass to the original dribbler behind their defender. Mission accomplished: The ball is in your team's possession and your teammate is behind their defender *(see Figure 2.6)*.

A few factors make a give-and-go (also called a one-two or a wall pass) work. First, the dribbler must take the defender on like a 1 v 1. If the defender does not fear the 1 v 1 move, the defender can thwart the give-and-go by playing the pass or the dribbler's run after the pass (the give). The dribbler's teammate must get into a position where the dribbler has an open passing lane. The dribbler needs to pass the ball to the teammate as efficiently as possible. Using the outside of the foot nearest the teammate is the most effective way for this first pass to be made—and the pass should be to the teammate's lead foot. The teammate should one-touch the ball behind the dribbler's defender to complete the give-and-go. After the initial pass, the passer runs around the defender, at speed, on the opposite side of the defender as the teammate. Thus, the dribbler's teammate acts as a wall in the give-and-go.

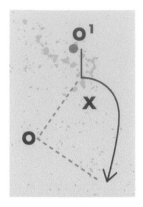

Figure 2.6

The give-and-go happens over and over again in matches and is one of the staples of the game. As a player, you need to perfect it as both the dribbler and the wall. Give-and-gos can occur in tight spaces or in more open parts of the field. Near the goal, the give-and-go is very effective at freeing a teammate for a shot. The closer to the goal, though, the tighter the give-and-go needs to be.

> As the receiver of the first pass (the wall), it is imperative that you do not hide behind the dribbler's defender. Give the dribbler that open passing lane and your success rate will be high.

Look for 1 v 1 Opportunities

Possession

If a defender has no help and you have the confidence, take that player on. If you beat your defender, then the entire defense of the opposing team has to alter their positions to recover due to your 1 v 1 success. You have broken down the defense.

Paying attention to spacing as a team will enhance your ability to get 1 v 1 situations. Teams on offense need to use both the depth and width of the field. Team defense is predicated on being compact in regard to depth and width. If your team can use the entire width of the field and stretch the defense by having a large distance from your backs to your strikers, your spacing will allow for better possession and many possible 1 v 1 situations.

When taking on your defender 1 v 1, try to keep your head up so you know where your teammates are positioned. Beating your defender 1 v 1 will force someone else's defender to come toward you. With your head up, you will be able to pass to that newly unmarked teammate, and you'll have further broken down the defense.

Teams need to take 1 v 1 chances to be more productive. Retaining possession will make your opponent chase and play defense longer. However, with two evenly matched teams, it is tough to break down defense with passing alone. Therefore, in the proper areas of the field and with a team trained to be confident taking people on 1 v 1, your team can be more productive while in possession of the ball.

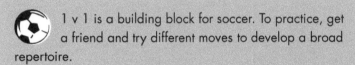

1 v 1 is a building block for soccer. To practice, get a friend and try different moves to develop a broad repertoire.

ALL YOU CAN DO IS PLAY
HOW YOU KNOW HOW TO PLAY.

—CLINT DEMPSEY

3 v 2 to Goal: Break Down the D

Attacking

When a 3 v 2 situation arises in a game, the offense has the advantage—and they should use that advantage quickly. You want to attack the defenders with speed because the two defenders will have teammates hustling back to help them. The longer it takes to be successful in a 3 v 2, the better the chances that other defenders will appear to thwart the goal-scoring opportunity. As in a 2 v 1 situation, always keep the 1 v 1 play in the mix. The defenders must respect the fact that you can beat them with a dribbling move. To do this, you need to isolate one of the two defenders, usually as one of the outside players, and beat the defender toward goal. In most cases, the other defender will come to you, opening up your two teammates for an open pass and a great chance at scoring a goal. Your teammates need to get in open passing lanes and be in a position to get a great shot *(see Figure 2.7)*.

If you're in the middle of the three, look to draw both defenders to you by trying to split them. However, be careful

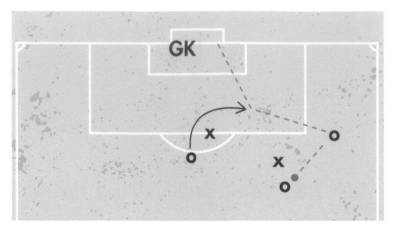

Figure 2.7

not to force the dribbling split; if you lose the ball, you have wasted a numerical advantage—something that doesn't present itself near the goal very often in an evenly played game. Forcing both defenders to come to you opens up your two teammates to receive passes and finish on goal or pass to the other teammate for an even better chance on goal.

Another way to be successful in the 3 v 2 is to attack at speed from the middle and get the ball to one of the two wing players—a player in a position to one touch a pass that splits the two defenders to the third player who receives the ball at speed with a great chance on goal.

> When doing a 3 v 2 exercise in training, it is imperative that you practice at game speed, as if more defenders are coming to help. If you do it slower than game speed, the drill becomes ineffective because it won't translate to a match.

Receive with a Purpose

Possession

In everything you do on the soccer field, you should have a purpose. Receiving the ball is no exception. There are many places on the field where you can receive the ball from your teammate. Finding a proper one might mean checking to a player to keep possession or to relieve the defensive pressure on your teammate with the ball. It could be to get in a position to spring your teammate on a give-and-go. It could be making a blind-sided run to get a leading pass to break down the defense toward goal. It might be making an overlapping run to open space for you and one of your teammates by unbalancing the defense.

How do you decide? First, you need to know what options you have. Then, through experience in matches and in training, learn what works in each situation. You also need to vary which runs you make so that your defender will not anticipate where you will go to receive the ball.

Lastly, you need to know what to do when you don't get a pass once you're in position to receive the ball. The main thing is to change your position to make your defender move and not stagnate your offense. The best move is to analyze where your next run to receive the ball has materialized and start the process again. This is the constant flow of the game—of adjusting and making decisions.

When watching games, try to key into a good player. See what runs the player makes and what receiving positions they get into. Ask yourself why the player did that, and try to determine where they may go next. The more you know about the game, the more you can incorporate into your own playing.

Triangle Support

Possession

When your team has the ball, it's important to give the player with the ball options. One good way to look at possession is to think of many triangles all over the field. When you have the ball, you are one of the points of the triangle. The other two players in the triangle provide support. As the ball moves, the players in the triangle move. When you have the ball at your feet, you may be in more than one triangle with different teammates. If you are a midfielder, you could have a triangle to your right, to your left, behind you, and in front of you. Being in the shape of a triangle provides depth and width. These triangles can be of different sizes and angles. No matter where the ball goes, players need to change their position to form new triangles.

Triangles reinforce the idea of moving off the ball. Since the ball is constantly moving, you and your teammates need to keep moving to adjust to its position. A player is very seldomly in a good position by staying in the same place when the ball changes position. Drastic position changes are not needed with

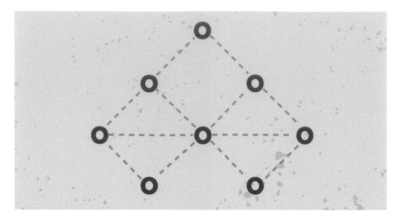

Figure 2.8

every movement of the ball, but players need to make adjust-
ments to be open to receive a pass while supporting their
teammate with the ball *(see Figure 2.8).*

To practice, train in a 3 v 2 keep-away drill—it requires you
to adjust your position with each movement of the ball. Obviously, you need to have good skills and great positioning to
retain the ball. You should make sure that you are in a position
to receive the ball and also to play the next pass. Many times, it
requires you to one-touch the ball. You should be constantly
thinking, "Where is the best position to keep possession of the
ball?" This 3 v 2 drill translates well into match situations.

> Getting into the right position to receive and then
> pass the ball is important. However, the most impor-
> tant thing is to have the skills to make the right play when you
> are in the right position. Keep improving your touch; it is a
> constant process.

14

Support Your Teammate with the Ball

Possession

When a teammate has the ball, you need to get in a position to support them so your team can keep possession. Remember: Your marking defender doesn't want to get beat and will therefore play defense to not allow you to get behind them. To keep possession, provide your teammate with a square-pass option or a back pass. It is always good if a player has multiple options to protect the ball *(see Figure 2.9)*.

To get in a square position to the teammate with the ball, put yourself at a 90-degree angle from the ball. Ideally, you want to be five to 10 yards away. If you are closer, the defender marking the ball may put more pressure on the ball, and your marking defender can potentially double-team the ball while still taking any pass to you out of the play. If you are too far away, your defender may be able to step up and steal the pass made to you.

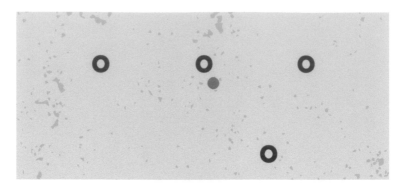

Figure 2.9

If you are supporting your teammate from behind, make sure that you verbally let your teammate know that you are there. A simple, "Behind you," can work. If you announce yourself, you must be open, since your teammate will not know where any defenders might be. Positionally, you need to be five or more yards behind your teammate. If you are closer than that, your teammate's marking defender may leave your teammate and close you down, putting you under pressure quickly.

If your defender is in a position to provide help defense or double-team your teammate, then you want to make a run to clear your defender out and open space for a teammate to be in a square position. Making your opponents chase defensively will help your team control the game. As a player in possession of the ball, you will want to have teammates support you so that you can make an easier pass.

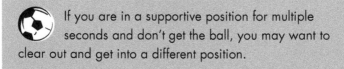
If you are in a supportive position for multiple seconds and don't get the ball, you may want to clear out and get into a different position.

Pass and Move

Possession

When your team has possession of the ball, it is important to pass and move. A stationary team is a team that can get a lot better. If you stay stationary after passing, you will be easily marked. However, if you move after passing, you are harder to mark, your defender has to pay attention to you, and your defender will be less likely to help defend another teammate.

There are situations, like a give-and-go, where it is imperative that the passer move after delivering the ball. Almost any pass could be a give-and-go, so a run behind your defender can yield a successful give-and-go. These runs don't always have to be fast, but they should be strategic. Runs should take your defender's eyes off the ball, so blind-sided runs are a good tactic. After passing, a run to open space for a teammate is often effective.

Even if you are passing to keep possession, a move to a slightly different position can open some space and put you in a more open passing lane. This is true with a back when passing

65

the ball to another back or midfielder. If you pass the ball to a midfielder, the striker that was marking you will turn to help defend the ball—and good players will run in the ball's recent path so as to not allow a return pass. If you move to another spot, you have opened a passing lane as the retreating striker can't see you and the ball at the same time.

Passing and then moving keeps defenders moving, too. If you can take a defender out of position or get yourself open, you have helped your team get better. Defensive players like to stay compact and stay in position. Passing and moving can force defenders out of position and stretch the defense.

> If you are stationary on the field, then your defender is stationary. If your team is stationary on the field, then the defense is stationary. Stationary is to the benefit of the defense. Pass and move to change that.

Attacking from the Flank: Be Dangerous

Scoring

As in war, the flank in a soccer game is the outside edge—the sideline. The most common players that would attack the flank are an outside striker, outside midfielder, or outside defender. Many people think that flank play will result in a cross—and it may. But there is more to attacking from the flank than simply producing crosses *(see Figure 2.10)*.

Starting with crosses, there is an early cross—one you can make from 20 yards or more from the end line. The early cross must be to the back post, and you need to make sure that you have teammates that can get to the ball (and not be in an offside position when you kick the cross). A more efficient cross is a later cross—one where you take the ball closer to the end line and deliver the ball to the near post with a driven ball, to the penalty spot with a lofted ball, or to the far post with a lofted ball.

67

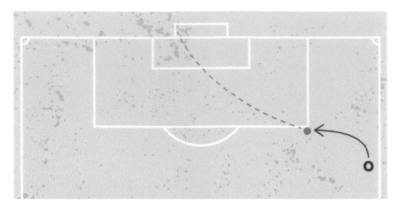

Figure 2.10

Now for the noncross moves from the flank. When carrying the ball to the end line, if you are facing a 1 v 1, you can attack the defender by trying to beat the defender 1 v 1 down the line toward the near post. Even if you lose the ball, your team should get a corner kick. Carrying the ball closer to the post means that the goalkeeper must protect the near post. This leaves your teammates in front of an open goal—one they can easily shoot toward if you send them a good pass on the ground.

Another noncross move is to cut back across the field around the top of the penalty area. You can then take a shot with the inside of the foot, curling it to the back post in the air—a very difficult ball for the goalkeeper to save.

> When attacking a defender from the flank, do it with speed. Remember: Your defender doesn't want to get beat toward the goal, so you should have an open path down the flank.

17

5 v 2: Make It Worthwhile

Possession

The 5 v 2 is a fun way to develop your passing skills as well as your thought process about the game. Many a coach will use 5 v 2 as a warm-up leading into practice. Briefly, it is five offensive players against two defenders in a confined area. The better the players, the smaller the space. The five play keep-away with the ball while the two try to win the ball or knock it out of the playing area. Usually, if one of the two defenders wins the ball or knocks it out of the area, they become part of the five and the person that lost possession becomes a defender *(see Figure 2.11)*.

Offensively, players want to move so that they can receive a pass with a passing lane to another player. Therefore, all five offensive players should adjust their position as the ball and players move. A 5 v 2 drill can be made more difficult by narrowing the size of the playing area or placing restrictions on the number of touches a player can take to pass the ball.

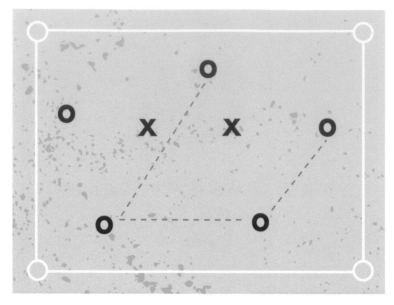

Figure 2.11

Positioning is imperative if you play a maximum of two touches each time a player plays the ball offensively. Getting open is one thing, but getting open and having a passing option is quite another. To keep yourself from having to play defense, you should always be thinking a couple of passes ahead. The exercise becomes even harder when you are allowed only one touch. Learning 5 v 2 will make you a better player in matches if you can transfer your movement in this smaller area to the big game field. (You can also think of the game field as made up of many smaller areas.)

One derivation of 5 v 2 that I like brings dribbling and quick feet into the equation. The restriction is that each offensive player *has* to touch the ball at least five times.

While the playing space is larger, players must dribble and then find a pass after their touches. You should try to keep your head up while dribbling to be able to release the ball to a teammate.

 Use your skills and positioning to keep yourself from playing defense. Learn what works and then do it. You will find that it will make you a better player.

YOU CAN EITHER STICK TO YOUR GOALS, OR YOU CAN JUST GO THROUGH THE MOTIONS AND REST ON YOUR STATUS. BUT IT'S ALL ABOUT WORK.

—KRISTINE LILLY

Keep Possession with Bent Ball Passes

Possession

Passing balls that curl can enhance your team's possession and efficiency. Becoming adept at this kind of passing will improve your game.

One of the ways that playing a bent ball to a teammate can be effective is placing a ball in front of the goal. If you are running with the ball and there is a defender between you and your teammate, you can use the inside of your foot to bend the ball so that it eludes the defender then curls toward your teammate. It is easier to play a ball back where it came from than make it change directions. Therefore, the curl on the ball will give your teammate trying to score a better angle on the ball than a straight pass at a 90-degree angle (across the shooter's body). Thanks to your bent pass, your teammate has an easier ball to play, thus increasing your teammate's chances of scoring.

If you have a lengthy pass to make to a teammate making a run near the sideline, you can bend the ball with either the inside or outside of your foot. The curl on the ball keeps it in play and your teammate can run into the ball. If you make a straight pass, your timing, pace, and accuracy have to be perfect to free up your teammate. Doing this increases your chances of completing this long pass and breaking down the defense.

Lastly, bending a ball around a defender who is in a direct passing lane allows you to make a successful pass even while the defender is in good position. This will enhance your team's possession and success.

> Learn to use all parts of your foot to strike the ball. Work on accuracy when bending the ball to make yourself a more formidable player.

Get in Defensive
1 v 1½ Situations

Defending

Individual defense is both physically challenging and mentally taxing—you don't want to get beat and everyone watching will know that you have been. So, you want to increase your chances for success, as well as help your teammates' individual defense. In 1 v 1 situations, you want to have help (support) on defense. This makes you a better defender, and this is where you look for 1 v 1½ situations *(see Figure 2.12)*.

A 1 v 1½ situation is created when you have a teammate in close proximity—one who can help you if you get beat by the offensive player. The offensive player could be in a position for a square pass. This second defender should be concerned with their mark first, but secondly with helping you. If your teammate's mark is in a position where they are unlikely to get open with a chance on goal, they might step up and help you if you get beat on the dribble. Your teammate should verbally let you

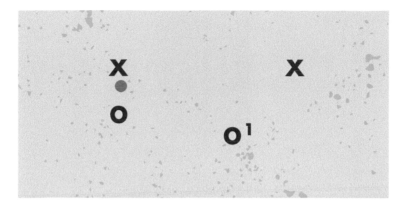

Figure 2.11

know that you have help on the right or left. Then you, as the first defender, need to change your positioning to shut off the opposite side. For example, if your teammate is on your right, you shut off the left by positioning your body to the left of your opponent. The dribbler is now channeled toward your team mate, and you can be more aggressive defending your mark. This will make you a better defender.

If you are near the sideline while defending 1 v 1, you can force your mark toward the sideline. The sideline becomes your ½ of the 1½. One thing the sideline never does is get beat; if the ball goes over the touchline, your team gets the ball.

> Communication is so important in defense. Ideally, the person that talks is the player that can see everything in the situation. In this case, it is your help defender. That player can see you, your mark, their mark, and the ball at the same time.

TACTIC

20

Space-Opening Runs

Possession

College golf is an individual sport played as a team, but soccer is a team sport played by individuals. What makes the difference in a team being successful is how teammates connect with one another. Players should dribble when it is best for the team. Players should shoot when it is best for the team. Players should pass when . . . you get the idea *(see Figure 2.12)*.

There are other, more subtle situations that happen on the pitch. One is dummying the ball to, hopefully, get it to a teammate who is in a better position than you are. This—like passing, shooting, and dribbling—is something easily noticed by the people watching the match. One thing that is less easily noticed is a player who makes runs to open space for a teammate.

As a productive player, you must read the game and help your team succeed. In this scenario, a teammate is making a run down the flank and has lost their defender. You are in the space where your teammate could receive a pass and be

76

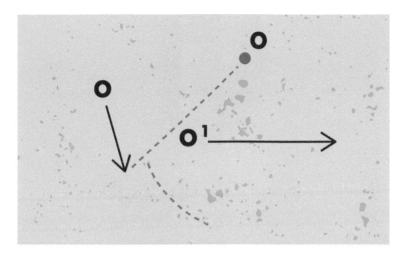

Figure 2.12

dangerous. However, if you stand there, your marking opponent could leave you to either steal that pass or defend your teammate. These kinds of situations require an unselfish player opening space. Before any pass is made, you make a run away from where your teammate would receive the ball—a dynamic run that your marking defender must respect. That defender will, more likely than not, follow you—or be distracted by your run, opening the flank for your open teammate.

Space opening runs can make your team better. You need to have knowledge of the game and think of what will happen ahead. A simple run across the defense can turn an average offensive opportunity into a dangerous opportunity.

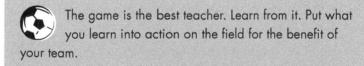 The game is the best teacher. Learn from it. Put what you learn into action on the field for the benefit of your team.

Attacking the Wall

Scoring

When your team gets a free kick outside of the penalty area but close enough for your opponent to worry about the prospect of a direct shot on goal, they will set up a wall. The first thing you should do is put the ball down at the spot of the foul. As the wall is being set, see whether someone can take a direct shot on goal quickly, because the goalkeeper is out of position. Also, check if you have an onside teammate that you can pass to—one who would be in a very dangerous position. Remember: Unless you ask the referee to step off 10 yards from the ball to the defense, you do not need another whistle after the foul has been called. If you are successful with a quick restart and score a goal, you will be glad that you placed the ball at the spot of the foul, so the referee doesn't call the goal back due to improper placement of the ball *(see Figure 2.13)*.

If neither of the quick restart options is open, you'll have to try to score against the wall and the goalkeeper. A properly placed wall will protect the near post, leaving the rest of the

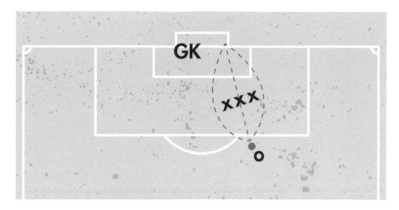

Figure 2.13

goal for the goalkeeper to defend. You may shoot the ball directly, but a straight shot will usually be saved by the goalkeeper or blocked by the wall. Kicking directly is enhanced by curling or dipping to the near post.

Rather than shooting directly, you may have a teammate tap the ball to either side to give you an angle to shoot behind the wall to the near post. This tap to the left or right needs to be done precisely, leaving the goalkeeper little time to adjust.

Lastly, it is good to have movement over the ball by teammates. For instance, a teammate can run over the ball to the outside of the wall. They may be unmarked, leaving them open for a firm pass. A defender may leave the wall to cover this runner, leaving the near post open for a shot.

> Movement by two or three people around the ball makes it difficult for the goalkeeper to predict who will take a shot—or whether you might try to spring a teammate free on the outside of the wall. Confusion is always to the advantage of the offense.

— TACTIC —

Pressure the Ball

Defense

Defensively, there is nothing more important than pressuring the ball. With proper pressuring, your opponent's options become limited. The player pressuring the ball needs to get as close to the player with the ball as they can without getting beaten. When pressuring a very talented player, give them a little more room. The opposite is true when defending a less proficient player: You should get in that player's grill, as tight as you can get. Either way, you don't want to get beat off the dribble or with a combination play, and you should adjust your position when playing against a very fast player.

As a player pressuring the ball, you want to take away opportunities for penetrating forward passes. The closer you can defend and not get beat off the dribble, the better. This allows the player to only pass the ball squarely or back. These kinds of passes do not break down your defense. Hopefully, after a square pass, one of your teammates will pressure the ball properly and only allow square and back passes. If your team can continue to pressure the ball and only allow square or back passes, your opponent will not be dangerous.

Remember: Do not get beat behind. If you dive in to steal the ball and you come up empty, your entire defense must adjust to make up for your overshot. Be solid defensively by pressuring the ball properly and your team will be a better team.

Playing 1 v 1 will help you get better at pressuring the ball by showing you how tightly you can cover your mark without getting beaten. Be light on your feet and strong with your upper body, and you can be a great 1 v 1 defender.

Support on Defense

Defense

After the pressuring defender, the support defender is the next most important defender on the field. This position is called a second defender, and there may be more than one in any given situation. As a support defender, your mark is one pass removed from getting the ball—and is usually in a square position in relationship to the player with the ball. Your job is to help the pressuring defender by being close enough to pressure your mark when the ball comes to them, and also to help the pressuring defender if they get beat. Positionally, you drop away from your mark and get in a position to tackle the pressuring defender's mark if your teammate gets beat on the dribble. Remember: You still need to be able to pressure the ball if it is passed to your mark.

Your positioning alone can make your pressuring teammate a better defender. When you're in a good helping position, let your teammate know, verbally, that they have support. Be specific, saying "help right" if you're to their right, and so on.

When the pressuring defender knows that there is help, they can channel their mark to you while cutting off the other side. With good positioning, you become an extra half defender for your teammate. Having help can also make a pressuring defender feel more comfortable to step a little tighter to the mark.

Sometimes, there may be two supporting defenders, one on each side. In this scenario, the pressuring defender can step hard to the ball and pressure the mark to make a mistake. If you work as a team and give good vocal instructions, every player on the field can be a better 1 v 1 defender.

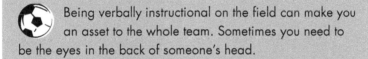

Being verbally instructional on the field can make you an asset to the whole team. Sometimes you need to be the eyes in the back of someone's head.

Defensive Cover

Defense

When you are on defense and more than one pass away from the ball, your role is to be a cover defender. This does not mean you cover your mark, but you cover for your teammates. Even so, you still need to stay close enough to your mark that you can get to them to pressure the ball when it is received.

To be a cover defender—and there can be multiple cover defenders at the same time—you are looking for dangerous areas and/or players. For instance, there might be a player advanced of the ball making a run, so you put yourself in a position to help out if the ball goes to that offensive player. Or the opponent may put a long ball into space deep down the field. You want to be able to help if that happens. You need to be close enough to your mark to pressure the ball if your mark receives it, but also in a position to help cover for other teammates.

If your mark is on the flank advanced of the ball and the ball is on the other side of the field, you would move more central and deeper to provide help as needed. You do not want to be deeper than the last line of defense. If the ball leaves the opposite flank and moves to the middle of the field, you will need to move nearer to your mark as they may be able to get the ball in fewer passes, thus taking less time to get there. You still cover, but you can't go as far into the middle of the field or as deep as before.

Ultimately, as a cover defender, your duty is to read the game and anticipate where the other team could become dangerous near your position on the field. You then alter your position as the ball moves. You are a helper until you become a support defender or a pressuring defender.

When watching games, note how players in positions similar to yours adjust depending on where their mark is and where the ball is at that time.

TACTIC

Stretch the Defense

Possession

As an offensive player, your positioning and movement can help your team possess the ball even when you are not physically playing it. When on offense, your team wants to stretch the defense from side to side and end to end. The more your team can stretch the defense, the more time and space each player will have when they receive the ball *(see Figure 2.14)*.

If you are a flank player and your team has the ball, you want to play near the touchline. If your defender moves to cover, then you need to move somewhere on the flank where your opponent's attention to the ball is altered by your movement. If you are a front runner (striker), it is your responsibility to stretch the defense from end to end (depth). You do this by moving further up the field and positioning as far forward as the defense will allow. Sometimes you can open up more space by running behind the defense in an offside position, tempting them to come back and guard you. Of course, you must be in an onside position if and when the ball is played to you.

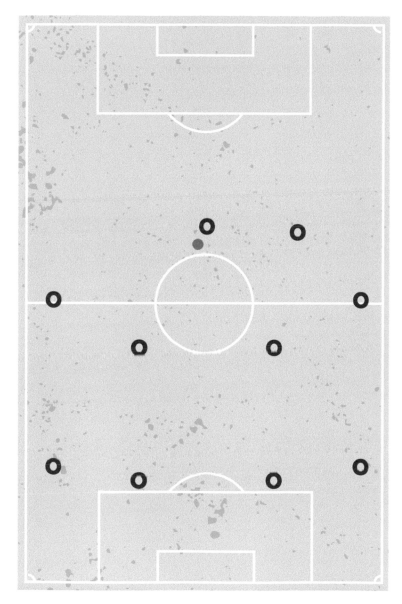

Figure 2.14

The idea of stretching the defense from touchline to touch-line and providing distance from the strikers to the defenders when you have the ball is to give the players in the middle of the field, where there are more players, more space and time to make things happen offensively. Possession becomes easier and penetrating passing angles are more prevalent when you can take the opponent's defense out of their compact positioning. It will also give you and your teammates more space and options to check to the ball, as well as reduce the number of times that an opponent's pressuring defender has a support defender. Making space by stretching the field will make your offense better.

> You can help your team offensively by positioning yourself and making runs that don't allow the defense much support or cover.

TACTIC

26

LEVEL

Penalty Kicks:
Hit Them Hard and Low

Scoring

When a penalty kick is called, the offensive team has a great chance to score. In fact, not scoring on a penalty kick can be a morale crusher for your team and a motivator for your opponent. The penalty kick on an 11 v 11 field is taken 12 yards from the goal line. The coach picks a player that has shown the ability to make a penalty kick. The kicker must have continuous movement forward and then take the kick. The goalkeeper must keep their feet on the goal line until the ball is kicked. However, the goalkeeper can move from side to side before the kick, as long as their feet remain on the line *(see Figure 2.15)*.

Some goalkeepers guess which way the ball will be kicked and dive that way as the kicker takes the shot. Others watch the kicker and try to see whether the kicker tips off where the ball will be kicked. When you're the kicker, you don't want to

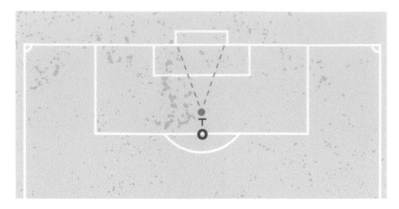

Figure 2.15

tip off the goalkeeper by opening your body too early so that you can only kick the ball to one side.

Practice kicking the ball with your stronger foot so that you can hit either corner or side-netting off the goal. You don't want to try to roof the ball (hit the ball high so it makes contact with the top of the net). This kind of shot gives you little margin of error, and balls over the goal can happen. The safer place is a well struck ball on or near the ground, requiring the goalkeeper to dive to make the save.

Mentally, you want to step up to the ball with confidence and know which side of the goal you are going to hit. Strike it confidently and with power.

Remember: If you hit a penalty kick and it hits the post or the crossbar and returns to you, it is illegal to play the ball. However, if the goalkeeper makes the save and allows a rebound, you may play that ball again.

TACTIC

Defending Close-in Indirect Kicks

Possession

When your team is defending a close-in (inside 10 yards) indirect kick in front of the goal, it is all hands on deck. Every player must get to the goal line as quickly as possible. While the other players line up, one player should be in front of the ball a few yards away to allow teammates to get back. If you are in front of the ball, be aware that the referee can give you a caution if you don't move away from the ball in a timely fashion *(see Figure 2.16)*.

All 11 players on your team will be on the goal line. If the ball is in the middle of the field, the goalkeeper should be on the goal line with five teammates on either side forming two walls. The two walls should give the goalkeeper space, maybe two yards between the ends of the walls. Since it is an indirect kick, two players must touch the ball. Usually, the offense will tap it to one side or the other. When the ball is tapped, one or two players in each wall will run at the ball in an attempt to snuff the shot, keeping their legs close together to not allow

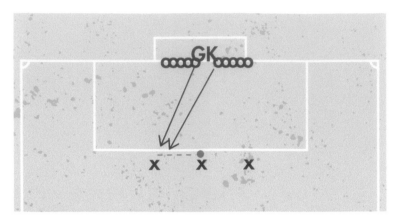

Figure 2.16

the ball through. The other four or five players in each wall stay together, taking a hop out from the goal to make it a more difficult angle for a player to put the ball into the goal. The goalkeeper should take a step forward on the pass to cut down the angle and then get set to face the shot.

Many times, the ball hits someone after the shot and becomes a loose ball in a dangerous position in front of the net. It is the responsibility of any and all defenders to clear the ball to safety. As goalkeeper, you should direct your defenders to attack the ball and any open attackers while still being prepared to make the save on any shot.

> On the initial pass, it can be enticing for a goalkeeper to charge the ball. Sometimes, this is effective. However, if the ball gets deflected and becomes loose in front of the net, the goalkeeper is out of position to make the play. Make sure you direct your teammates to the most dangerous areas.

TACTIC

28

Long Free Kicks

Scoring

When you have a long free kick (from midfield to 35 yards from the goal) from the center of the field, you want to make it dangerous. Many teams will set a line of defense to allow space for the goalkeeper to come out and win the ball. Many times, that line is on the 18-yard line—the top of the penalty area. As the kicker, you want to get the ball over that line of defense, making the defenders turn and face their own goal. Doing this will make clearing the ball a much tougher assignment. Your players should be running toward the goal when you kick the ball, thus staying onside. Players should attempt to get a piece of the ball with their heads or other body parts. The ball needs to be in front of the net, but short enough that the goalkeeper has to avoid running into defenders and your teammates to play the ball with hands *(see Figure 2.17)*.

If you don't clear the line of defense with your kick, you are setting up your opponent's counterattack. Since your teammates are expecting you to hit a great ball, they are running

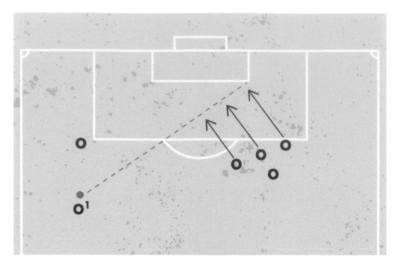

Figure 2.17

quickly into the box. The defenders will see your short kick before your teammates do, making it easy for them to play the ball the way they face before your teammates turn to chase them down. Your kick is critical to your team's success.

If you are taking a long free kick from an angle, place the ball over the line of defense, look for the ball to go to the back post, and make sure you take the goalkeeper out of play (don't hit it to the goalkeeper). Hitting the ball to the back post area both gives your teammates time to get to that position and makes the goalkeeper move across the goal. A shot or pass to the back post will be very dangerous.

Your team should make sure that there are players in front of the goal at the far post, the center, and the near post. They can play the initial ball from you, as well as second or third balls from teammates or off errant clears by the defenders.

Offensive Indirect Free Kicks

Scoring

When an indirect foul is called against your opponent, you will be awarded an indirect free kick. If that kick is 10 or more yards away from your goal and in a dangerous shooting position, you need a plan to increase your chances of scoring. Your opponent will set up a wall to protect the near post, while the goalkeeper will be in position to protect the goal nearer the back post.

The goal of taking the kick is to score in two touches. To do this, make a square pass to a teammate a couple of yards away, either to the inside or outside of the wall. It is good to have a teammate on either side so that the defense and goalkeeper will not know where the shot is coming from. The player who receives that pass then takes a driven shot to the area where the wall was protecting the goal. If your pass goes to the outside, the wall is now protecting the back post and the goalkeeper will move to protect the near post. If the shot is taken quickly, the goalkeeper will not be set and will be more vulnerable. If your pass goes to the inside of the wall, the goalkeeper cannot move across the goal because, if he does, the back post is now open.

Most defenses will have the player on the inside end of the wall run at the ball once you have touched it to a teammate. This makes it vitally important to pass and shoot very quickly.

> You may want to have a teammate run over the ball and make a run outside of the wall. This may cause the player on the end of the wall to move, giving the shooter more of a target. Also, being deceptive with your pass may keep the goalkeeper guessing about who will do the shooting.

ENTHUSIASM IS EVERYTHING. IT MUST BE TAUT AND VIBRATING LIKE A GUITAR STRING.

—PELÉ

Learn Your Opponent

Defense

When you are playing in a match, you often won't know much about the opposition except for their record or place in the standings. When it comes to individual players, you may know very little. The game itself becomes a learning experience. When watching a match on television, you might hear the announcer talk about teams feeling one another out. Overall, as a team, your opponent may like to attack the flank, play long balls, possess from the back, punt each time, etc. Whatever their tendencies and abilities, you need to figure them out.

As an individual player, your task is to learn the tendencies of players that you will mark or that will mark you. To do this, you may want to be cautious when one of your marks gets the ball early in a match. Your mark could be extremely fast or very adept with the ball. Your mark could be lacking in some skills. After one or two encounters with your mark, you should have some idea of their ability with the ball, how fast they are, and which foot is stronger. Each of these items will help you guard your opponent better as the game goes on. Don't simply assume that a player has certain assets and deficiencies. It is better to err on the side of caution.

Once you determine the quality of your opponent, make decisions that will help you be productive on the field. If a player isn't as skilled, pressure the ball tighter. If the player is fast, give yourself more room defending. If the player is one-footed, force them to the weak side.

When you have the ball, you also need to figure out the relative strengths and weaknesses of your opponent's defense. If a player doesn't defend well in 1 v 1 situations, take them on. Look for clues. See the best way to win these individual battles.

> After a game, your coach should be able to get an intelligent answer from you about the relative strengths and weaknesses of your marks. Learn from each and every game.

31

Goalkeeping Positioning: Know Your Angles

Goalkeeping

Goalkeepers are a big 1/11 of a team. For the most part, they don't have the same array of skills that their field-playing teammates do. As everyone knows, the goalkeepers have special benefits. They wear a different uniform, are allowed to use their hands in the penalty area, and can't be charged (legally) by a field player in their goal box. But they are a big 1/11 because they protect the goal *(see Figure 2.18)*.

Despite being alone many times during the game, goalkeeper positioning is a full time exercise in every game. Most everyone knows that goalkeepers need to be in good position when the opponent is shooting on goal. Put simply, you need to protect the near post and cut down the angle of the shot by getting off your line (goal line between the posts). If a player comes at you from an angle, you need to position yourself in front of the post. Many shots will come at you hard toward the

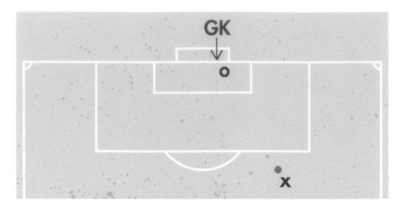

Figure 2.18

near post, and if your parry the ball, you want it to go out for a corner kick instead of into the goal.

When the ball is in midfield or at the other end of the field, the goalkeeper positioning continues to be important. At all times, you should be between the ball and the center of your goal. Where the ball is and which team has possession will determine how far off your line you should be. This, many times, will be outside of the penalty area. Always be ready to thwart a chance by coming out of the penalty area and playing a ball, either to clear or pass to a teammate.

Goalkeepers also need to be the extra back when their team is working the ball out of the back. Depending on your coach's wishes, goalkeepers need to stay central in the field and have good ball skills. This can allow your team to free up an extra player, making your team more dangerous offensively.

Some goalkeepers think it is good enough to be a shot blocker, but they're wrong. The goalkeeper starts the offense and anchors the defense. Goalkeepers need to train to become very good with their feet and play the ball.

Start the Offense as a Goalkeeper: Dead Balls

Goalkeeping

As a goalkeeper, you are not only the last line of defense—you are also the initiator of the offense. Once you control the ball with your hands in the run of play, you have six seconds to put it back in play. It is a misconception that punts and dropkicks should be hit as far as you can hit the ball. A long time in the air and randomness in direction make those long and high balls 50-50 opportunities at best, since they give the defense a chance to play the ball the way they are facing. Therefore, goalkeepers should hit punts and dropkicks to an open player and keep the ball on a lower trajectory so that it gets to your aiming spot faster. This increases your team's chances of possessing the ball.

When taking goal kicks, you want to try to keep possession of the ball for your team. If you are kicking the ball long, place it on the goal box line six yards from the goal in the center of the pitch. This way, you can be in position in case there's a poor kick or an opponent wins the ball and the other team attacks immediately. The ball needs to be high enough to clear the first line of defense, but driven so it gets to your teammate as quickly as possible. Just as with punts and dropkicks, you want to increase your chances of possessing the ball by hitting it to an open player as quickly as possible.

On goal kicks, you also may start the possession by making the first pass from the back. The majority of time, it is a pass to your wing defender who is on the flank outside the penalty area. Of course, do not pass this ball to a player who is closely defended. After you take the short goal kick, be ready to support your teammate as the ball may need to be returned to you. Then, play as a field player and help build the ball from the back.

As a goalkeeper, you need to be able to play the ball with your feet during the run of play. You can contribute to the success of your team by making firm and accurate passes that start possession for your team. Get good with your feet and you will be a better goalkeeper.

Start the Offense as a Goalkeeper: Balls in Play

Goalkeeping

When the ball is in play and you get a pass from your teammate, you cannot pick up the ball; you must use your feet. Sometimes, you will be under immediate pressure and will need to clear the ball. In these situations, make sure that you know where your teammates are so that you can clear the ball in their direction. If you are not under defensive pressure, keep possession by passing to an open teammate. Many times, you are the conduit for changing the point of attack from one side to the other.

When you have controlled the ball with your hands and want to keep possession, using a throw or a roll (bowling technique) can easily do the trick. For short passes, rolling the ball is the most effective way to get it to your teammate. Roll the ball at pace, and keep it on the ground so it is easier for your teammate to play. Sometimes, you will roll to your teammate's feet or make a pass to lead your teammate. This is done on the flank, where there are not as many defenders. Making a good pass is imperative. It is bad enough to allow a goal—but allowing a goal due to a bad pass that you made is even worse.

The best way for you to keep possession on intermediate distance passes is to throw the ball. To be clear, you don't want to throw the ball like a baseball. Instead, cup the ball with your hand and, with a straight arm, throw the ball directly over your head. Try to get the ball to a teammate's feet so that your team can keep possession.

In any of these situations, it is important for you to make a decision quickly about where to deliver the ball. The longer you wait, the more time your opponent has to get back and set up their defense, thus making a successful distribution tougher.

> Distribution is an important part of goalkeeping. Practice drills that stress possession with your teammates. Train to be accurate with your throws and rolls.

34

Goalkeeper Playing Crosses: Remember Cinderella

Goalkeeping

A cross during the run of play or on a corner kick is a dangerous opportunity. Goalkeeper positioning and timing is very important on crosses. On a corner kick, the defense is set whether your team plays man-to-man, zone, or a zone/man-to-man hybrid. On the reverse side, your opponent will have corner kick plays. The goalkeeper needs to set the defense and alert them about who is the most dangerous and ensure the right matchups, usually based on height. As a goalkeeper, your positioning on a corner should be near your goal line, facing the ball, typically nearer the back post than the near post. It is much easier to run forward on a ball than to backpedal. When the ball is in the air, you should be a force. Assess the flight of the ball and decide whether you can get it in the air. If you can, then come out dynamically and use your hands—which give you quite a height advantage over other players.

But when should you come out for the ball? *Whenever you can get it!* But do be sure. If you commit to coming out and then don't get the ball, you have left the goal wide open, thus increasing your opponent's chance of scoring. To do this, you need patience. Think of the Cinderella Principle, which is arrive late to the ball. If you go early, many things can change in front of you, and you may end up in no man's land. You don't want to be there.

A cross during the run of play is similar to a corner except not a set play, and the ball is not often served from the end line. You need to have your head on a swivel and help your teammates find their marks because you don't want an open header. Your positioning will depend on where the ball is served, how many opponents will have a chance to score, and how many of your teammates are back to defend. With all that, the goalkeeper then plays the cross like a corner.

Goalkeepers need to work on crosses in training and catch the ball at its highest reachable height, where they have the advantage. If a goalkeeper catches a ball at head height, the opponent has as good of a chance to play the ball as the goalkeeper. You have an advantage. Use it.

First-Time Finishing

Scoring

As you get older and more experienced, so do your opponents. As this happens, the speed of play increases, as do the speed and skill of the players. The offense is quicker, but the defense is better at thwarting it. One area where time and space are reduced is in your offensive penalty area. The defenders will seem to be everywhere. This makes it tougher to get a two-touch or more shot off. The defenders close you down, and the goalkeeper gets set in a good position, all of which make it tougher to score.

In these situations, it is good to be adept at first-time finishing. A quick first-time shot has a better chance of getting through the defense without being snuffed at the point of contact. You have a better chance of catching the goalkeeper out of position as they adjust position from the movement of the ball.

To hit the ball properly, you must be squared up to the ball when it reaches you. Do this by constantly changing your body position and making educated guesses where the ball might end up at your feet. You must be mentally ready. You must think that the ball will get to you, and you must be ready to strike it. Then, when a ball does get to you, you confidently strike it low and hard toward the goal. You might score directly. The ball may careen off a defender or a teammate and end up in the goal, or it could bounce out to you or another teammate who is ready to finish on the rebound. Readiness and position-ing are the keys to success.

Solid contact is important in scoring. In training, practice hitting balls quickly with one touch by doing the machine-gun drill. Line up many balls. Then, move across the line, and strike the balls hard at the goal as fast as you can. Do not step back to recover, just recoil and strike the ball.

TACTIC

36

Add Some Spice to Your Game: Nutmeg

Attacking

In almost all cases, the goal of attacking on the dribble is to beat your defender by going around them, then put yourself in a position so that the defender needs to go through you to get the ball. One of the more exciting moves on the pitch is when you nutmeg your defender—beat them through the legs *(see Figure 2.19)*.

To nutmeg your defender, you try to open their legs by making them reach for the ball and end up square to you (both feet being the same distance from the ball). With a quick touch of the ball through the wicket (legs), you accelerate past the flat-footed defender and get the ball on the other side of them. Then, you are off to the races. You might hear "olé" from your teammates or the sidelines. A good nutmeg is the epitome of successful dribbling moves. You will find that, after you nutmeg a player, you have more time with the ball the next time you are matched in a 1 v 1 situation with the same defender. The defender doesn't want to be humiliated by another nutmeg, so they give you more room.

Figure 2.19

When training, make sure you get plenty of practice controlling the ball in tight spaces. It is good to practice this in a 1 v 2 drill where losing the ball is expected. The quicker you are in dribbling possession, the more ways you can beat your defender.

The goal of dribbling is to beat the opponent and keep possession going down the pitch. Don't force fancy dribbling moves, as you might lose possession more often. However, you do need some of these moves in your repertoire in case the opportunity arises.

TACTIC

37

LEVEL

Dummy the Ball

Possession

A dummy happens when a player allows a ball to continue travelling without playing it. You see it done on corner kicks, where the near-post player lets the ball go by so that it can reach a teammate in better position. You may be marked tightly with limited options to make a penetrating pass. The ball's path would be where a good-to-great pass may go, so you let it go. If the ball would end up in a dangerous offensive position without you touching it, and you have a teammate in position and no defenders in the ball's path, go ahead and dummy it *(see Figure 2.20)*.

The key to a successful dummy is to make your defender think that you are going to play the ball. You must make sure that your defender is not in the path of the ball, because it may hit that defender inadvertently and thwart the play. As the ball is arriving, act as if you were going to receive the ball—just don't actually play it when it arrives.

111

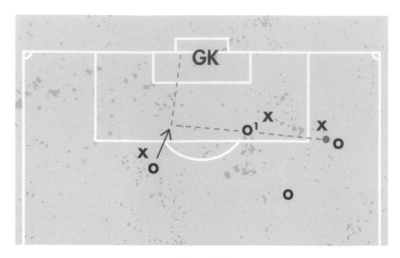

Figure 2.20

Since players tend to anticipate what an opponent might do, looking like you are going to play the ball usually stops another player from attacking defensively. You can also look like you are going to play a ball that will roll out of bounds to slow down the opponent. You might step over the ball one or more times while shielding to get a throw-in.

> Learn the game by always being thoughtful in practices and matches. The game is there to be learned, so take the initiative to learn from it.

Heading to Finish: Hit the Goal Line

Scoring

Scoring on a header is one of the most exciting plays in soccer. It is a difficult skill—and very seldom do you get an uncontested header in the penalty area. Even so, there are a few things that can help you score on a header.

First, the best place to finish on a header is away from the goalkeeper, toward the goal line. Most goalkeepers are good on high balls, but hitting the goal line makes the goalkeeper dive down to make the save. To head the ball downward, throw your eyes at the ball, and hit the ball with force. By throwing your eyes at the ball, your forehead will face down, thus aiming at the goal line. You should strike the ball above the center to propel it downward.

Many times, you will be marked as a ball comes to you. You need to be ball side and usually jump before your defender does. Using good heading technique and knocking the ball down will enhance your scoring odds. Keep your arms wide to achieve better balance.

When positioned on the near post, try to skim the ball to change its flight and put it on goal. Use the ball's own speed to your advantage. This requires the goalkeeper to react quickly, giving you a great chance to score directly or let the goalkeeper make a save with rebound potential.

If you are receiving an air ball on the back post, use the same technique. Unless the goalkeeper leaves your near post open (where you would hammer it there and start celebrating), you want to hit the ball at the back post. If it goes in, great; if it is saved and there is a rebound, the ball will stay in play, allowing your teammates to finish.

> Arriving at the spot of your header at the same time as the ball will make you harder for a defender to mark. Time your run, and you will earn some uncontested headers to finish.

39

Heading to Clear: Get It to Safety

Defending

As a defender, you will face long balls from your opponent. Sometimes, you will need to head those balls to clear them to safety. Heading to clear means heading the ball high and far, ideally in the direction of your teammate(s). As in heading to finish, you want to throw your eyes at the ball, only in this case your eyes will be facing the sky rather than the ground. Use proper heading technique to propel the ball *(see Figure 2.21)*.

When the opposition is crossing the ball in the penalty area from the flanks, you still need to hit the ball high and far to clear it. Make sure that the ball doesn't cross the goal-to-goal middle line of the field—the imaginary line that runs from the middle of one goal to the middle of the other goal. If you clear a ball across that line, you increase the odds of an opponent winning the ball and getting a chance on goal. So, what do you do? If you are on the near-post side of the imaginary line, head

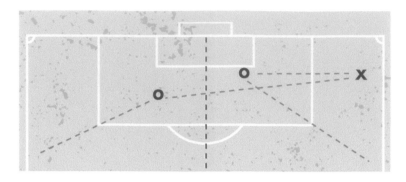

Figure 2.21

the ball back in the direction it came from, and hit it up the field. If you are on the far post of the imaginary line, keep the ball moving in the same direction, just up the field. Even poorly executed headers will usually stay out of trouble, but a poor header that travels toward that imaginary line is a bonus chance for your opponents.

When a long ball comes from your opposition from straight up the field, you may want to skim head the ball in the same direction back to your goalkeeper, who can then safely pick the ball up and start the offense from there. When skimming the ball, just barely hit the ball to keep its momentum. Most opponents who are coming to challenge your header will assume you will head it back from where it came from and will slow down, thus giving the ball time to reach the goalkeeper and the goalkeeper time to get to the ball.

> If you are a defender, it is imperative that you become a good header of the ball. You may want to practice technique with a slightly deflated ball, a Nerf ball, or something similar. There are now softer balls on the market that allow you to practice heading without risking injury.

Heading to Pass: Keep It

Possession

When heading to clear, in most cases, you head the ball high and long—away from danger and, hopefully, in the direction of some teammates. When you head to finish, you hope that no one plays the ball—except when the opposing goalkeeper picks the ball out of the net. Heading to pass, though, should be thought of as the same as a pass made with your foot.

Most times, when heading to pass, the pace of the ball off your head is as important as the direction the ball is heading (no pun intended). To slow the ball's pace, soften the ball by giving with your neck. When passing the ball with your head, try to aim the pass to your teammate's feet, making it easier to keep possession. Heading passes can be made to your teammates or back to your goalkeeper to maintain possession.

Experiment until you have a good sense of how to correctly control the direction and pace of a headed pass. Making one-touch passes with your foot isn't easy, and making a one-touch pass with your head is even more difficult. You become a more complete player by mastering all the skills with your head.

Remember: If you pass the ball with your head, it allows the goalkeeper to play the ball with their hands. Of course, that is not true if the ball is passed to the goalkeeper with your feet.

YOU HAVE TO FIGHT TO REACH YOUR DREAM.
YOU HAVE TO SACRIFICE AND WORK HARD FOR IT.
—LIONEL MESSI

41

Increasing Your Chances of Scoring

Scoring

As you mature as a player, so do your opponents. Defenders are better, and goalkeepers are quicker and cover more of the goal. What can you do to give yourself a better chance to score?

First and foremost, be ready to hit a quality shot with a first touch. Too many times, players fear a miss-hit on a one-touch shot. Quick first-time bent shots from a place where you can receive the ball have a great chance to score. While making a first touch to set up a second-touch shot may put you in a comfort zone, it also allows the defense to get in better positions. You have a better chance to score on a weak first-time shot than you do on a better second-touch shot.

Goalkeepers are taught to guard the near post. The reason for guarding the near post is that it is the shorter distance and therefore the easier shot to take. If the goalkeeper is in good position, shoot to the far post to score. Of course, this takes practice. A first-time shot to the back post can be very effective.

Also, learn to strike shots on goal from positions where you receive the ball. Anybody can shoot from the penalty spot. In reality though, it is tough for a player to get the ball there. Learn where you can realistically receive the ball, and practice scoring from there. When I was coaching in college, one of my players learned where he could receive the ball in games and practiced shooting from there. Many times, he would be out practicing well after the team practice ended. Despite not being overly talented, he ended up being the second-leading career scorer.

> Understand that shooting is a technique and scoring is a tactic that requires shooting in most cases. Ugly goals and short goals count just as much as 18-yard bicycle kicks. Learn how to score, and you will make an impact for your team.

TACTIC

LEVEL

Scoring on Close Indirect Kicks

Scoring

If an indirect foul is called inside the last 10 yards of the field in front of your goal, you will be awarded an indirect kick. By rule, an indirect kick cannot be taken closer than six yards away, no matter where the foul is called. If the foul is whistled inside the goal box, the indirect free kick is taken on the six-yard line that forms part of the goal box. In all other cases, the defensive wall must be 10 yards from the ball. However, since there are not 10 yards of space, all defensive players have to be 10 yards away or on the goal line. In these cases, most teams will have all 11 players on the goal line.

To attack this defensive wall setup, you need a plan. An indirect free kick taken from six to 10 yards in front of the goal should create a goal more often than not. With no plan though, many of these chances are wasted.

Scoring a goal will require you to first-touch the ball to a teammate. You should have your back to the goal and two to four teammates about two yards away ready to receive your

121

short pass. You will pass the ball back at an angle to give your teammate more time to shoot as the defenders rush the ball. Your teammate should shoot the ball quickly and at a high trajectory (at the defender's head height or higher but below the crossbar). The shooter should also aim the ball away from the goalkeeper, who will be on the line with teammates in the wall. After you make the pass, turn and be ready for any rebound. Your teammates should do the same.

Quickness and shot accuracy are the most important components of having a successful close-in indirect kick.

> If you are the player making the first pass, consider faking the pass to get the wall moving. As the defenders retreat, gaps in the wall emerge. However, your teammates must know your plan; otherwise they may not be ready to shoot.

FOR A GOALKEEPER, THERE IS NO HIDING PLACE.

—BRAD FRIEDEL

1 v 2: Test Yourself

Possession

When it comes to helping you become strong on the ball and able to hold off multiple defenders at the same time, practice makes perfect. To develop this skill, try this activity, which can be done in practice or with friends in a backyard or park.

The object is to keep the ball as the offensive player (the number 1 player of the 1 v 2) while being defended by two opponents (the number 2 of the 1 v 2) in a confined space of 8 by 8 to 10 by 10 yards. If you are the offensive player, try to protect and hold possession of the ball by shielding and making space for yourself by beating your opponents. Try to split the defenders, which will get you open for a brief time to do the same thing over again. As the outnumbered offensive player, you need to use all of this limited space to make time for yourself.

Keep the ball until one of the defenders steals it. Then, that player becomes the offensive player, and you join the other player in trying to win the ball back. If the ball goes out of the playing area off the offensive player, then the closest defender becomes the offensive player. If the ball is knocked out of the area by one of the defensive players, the offensive player retains possession.

This activity not only enhances your shielding ability, but it also helps you move from just shielding to actually beating your opponents. It tests your dribbling moves in a confined space and challenges you to split your defenders with a crafty and powerful move.

These 1 v 2 skirmishes need to be done in short bursts of 60 to 90 seconds, because they are very physically taxing. This kind of anaerobic activity will prepare you for the rigors of the game. Playing multiple sets of 1 v 2 will get you in shape, enhance your skills, and teach you how to set up your defenders for splitting them—making you more dangerous on the field.

1 v 1 is a great way to perfect your dribbling moves, but playing 1 v 2 more than doubles the intensity of 1 v 1. Keeping the ball at all costs in your backyard or in training will make you a more valuable player.

TACTIC

Tackle or Delay?

Defense

Tackle or delay? When you are closing down an opponent who just received the ball, this is a great question—one best answered by the situation. If you are a defender, your opponent puts a long penetrating pass to a player down the flank, and your outside back has been beaten, then in many cases, you want to delay. You are playing 1 v 1 with a player, who, if they beat you, will create a very good chance for your opponents. Give this player a little more room, and take away any chance of getting beat. You are ultimately delaying to allow your teammates a chance to get back, giving you numerical superiority in the final third. Your teammates should let you know to delay. On any team that I have coached, you would hear the team and the sidelines yelling not to dive (diving in trying to win the ball). You need to do whatever you do best to keep the ball and player from getting past you.

The more support you have on the field from teammates or the touchline, the better option tackling the ball may be. Before you tackle, you must make sure you are in a lowered position and ready to win the ball. You need to know which players are susceptible to being tackled. In games, you don't see defenders attempting to dispossess Lionel Messi or Cristiano Ronaldo of the ball because those two players can beat even the best of defenders. The only time those great players (and others like them) are tackled is when they are deep in the final third of the field, where defenders have no other choice.

It's always important to know the situation of the game, the relative strength of your opponent compared with you, and where your teammates are located on the field. Spatial awareness and knowledge of the game will help you answer the question.

> When delaying an opponent with the ball, make sure you know where other offensive players are on the field. You can then close down the player with an angle where a penetrating pass to an open opponent is more difficult. Doing this may make a very dangerous situation less dangerous.

MY LIFE IS TRAINING.

—TIM HOWARD

MENTAL
EXERCISES

There's no shame in running your hardest, even if you end up falling behind. But when you make a mental mistake? That's rough. Now that we've covered your physical skills and your on-field tactics, let's make sure you've got your head in the game.

Numbering of Positions

Formation

In today's game, positions are given a number. Instead of position names, many coaches simply use numbers. In this numbering system, the goalkeeper is number 1. Many goalkeepers wear number 1—a tradition that goes back to when teams would have the starting 11 players wear numbers 1 through 11 depending on their position. So, each game day, the players would wear the jersey bearing the number of their position *(see Figure 3.1)*.

Here, I will list the positions as though the team is playing a 4-3-3 (four backs, three midfielders, and three strikers)—sometimes referred to as a 1-4-3-3, counting the goalkeeper. The outside backs are numbers 2 and 3. The center backs are numbers 4 and 5. In today's game, the outside backs are as much offensive players as they are defensive players. The center backs can and do make runs forward. Even so, their duty is first as defenders, then starting the offense by working the ball out of the back.

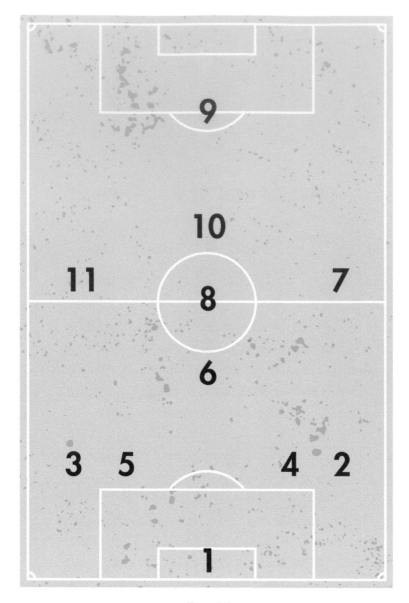

Figure 3.1

The number 6 is the defensive center midfielder or holding midfielder. If you play this position, both titles describe what you do. You are a midfielder, but you also have defensive responsibilities and stay in a holding position behind your team's other midfielders. The number 8 is the box-to-box center midfielder. If you play here, you will have roughly equal offensive and defensive responsibilities. You need to be fit to play from one penalty area to the other. The number 10 is the attacking center midfielder. As the name implies, you make things happen on the offensive end. On most soccer teams, the number 10 jersey is coveted. Some very great and creative players have worn number 10—Pelé and Messi to name a couple.

The wingers in the 4-3-3 are numbers 7 and 11. If you play a winger, your job is to attack the flank and make things happen offensively. The last player, number 9, is the central striker. If you play there, it is your job to score goals, to shield the ball as teammates run off you, and to be an intimidating offensive force on the field.

Learn these numbers. They'll come in handy if you ever have a coach or trainer who uses them. It is much better to understand what the coach is talking about than to try to figure it out on the field.

Outside Backs: Own the Flank

Read the Game

One of the many changes that has occurred in the modern game of soccer is the need for the goalkeeper to have field skills. This became imperative when the rules changed so that a pass to the goalkeeper was no longer allowed to be picked up (yes, that was a long time ago). As soccer became more of a possession game, defensive players (backs) also had to expand their skill sets. It became imperative for backs to develop offensive skills beyond their defensive responsibilities.

On most teams, the players that are asked to do the most are the outside backs. Coaches ask these players to own the flank and play from end line to end line—making them both defensive and offensive players. If you are an outside back, you need to be fit—ready to run more than any other player on the field. You need to be able to defend during 1 v 1 situations, since you will often be left without help on the flank. Offensively, you need to be able to carry the ball up the flank and serve balls into the box.

When watching games, notice that in many systems the outside backs are not involved early in working the ball from the back. The two central defenders—the goalkeeper and a holding midfielder—form the quartet that start working the ball from the back. Outside backs are stretching the field both in width and depth. The better the team, the more important it is to have great outside backs. As you watch games, concentrate on what the outside backs are doing in different situations. Watch how positioning shifts depending on where the ball is, and then notice what players do when the ball comes to them.

> Train like you will be an outside back. If you get moved to any other position (other than goalkeeper), your training will allow you to perform.

FOOTBALL IS A GAME YOU PLAY WITH YOUR MIND.
—JOHAN CRUYFF

The Back Four:
Defensive Positioning Is Key

Defense

If you are a member of the back four (i.e., the defenders), it is imperative to work as a unit in conjunction with the goalkeeper to keep the ball out of your net and begin possession of the ball offensively. An informative goalkeeper who can instruct the backs is a must. The goalkeeper can see the whole field and, with good instructions to the backs, minimize dangerous opportunities by the other team *(see Figure 3.2)*.

During the run of play, in an ideal scenario, there should be more backs than attacking offensive players. You want to have a defender mark the player with the ball while the two closest teammates provide defensive support. If the ball is in the center of the pitch, one of the central defenders pressures the ball while the other central defender and one of the outside backs provide support. The other outside defender supplies cover. If the ball is on the flank, the outside back provides pressure, while one center back provides support and the other two backs provide cover.

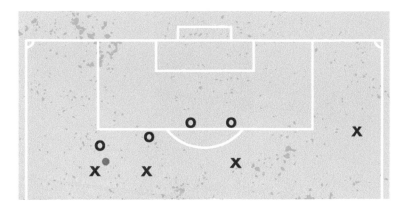

Figure 3.2

When winning the ball, the back four want to become part of your team's offense. If you win the ball in the run of play, you want to get it to an open teammate ahead of you when you can. Unless pressured, clearing the ball down the field will more than likely end up with the other team in possession (and you playing defense again). Also, when your team has the ball, the back four need to push up toward the center line to keep the opponent from getting space in your defensive half of the field. This can cause the lazy attacker to be offside. However, pushing up must be done as a unit, otherwise that lazy (or opportunistic) attacker can take advantage due to one of the back four not pushing up (i.e., a lazy defender). The back four move up as a unit—or not at all.

When watching games, pay attention to how the back four work as a unit. A good back four know where the other three are, and they move as a unit to make it difficult for the opponent to get good chances. Keep learning from others.

Width and Depth: Offense

Possession

If you are on offense, spreading the field out will open up passing lanes and give players more time and space with the ball. Of course, your team needs great skills, but having extra time and space never hurts (at least not the offense).

To spread out the field, your team needs both width (from sideline to sideline) and depth (from end to end). Your outside players need to be close to the touchline but not close to one another. Your central defenders need to drop back far enough to give your midfielders and strikers an option to pass the ball back to them. The goalkeeper (yes, the goalkeeper on offense) needs to be a secondary option for passing the ball back to retain possession and restart the offense. The strikers need to push forward as much as the defense allows to further stretch the field. Most defenses will push up to compact their team, but strikers need to constantly change their position. It is a good tactic for strikers to play behind the defenders, in an offside position, when they know that a pass will not be coming to them. This forces the defenders to adjust their position.

You and your teammates now need to move the ball and your positioning. As players leave one spot on the field to check to the ball to receive it, another player should fill the newly opened position. The checking player leaves a vacuum (an open space), and another player fills that space. Of course, the player that filled that space opened another vacuum that can also be filled by one of your teammates. This constant movement—the getting open, filling spaces, and getting open again—will make your team that much harder to defend. Looking for ways to create time and space for yourself will make you a better player when you receive the ball.

> Remember to time your runs and be a good target for your teammate. If you are standing, you are much easier to mark than if you are moving. Move with purpose.

MENTAL
EXERCISE

Width and Depth: Defense

Defense

When your team is playing defense, it helps to know the principles of depth and width defensively. When playing defense, the object of formation is to be as compact as possible. This will help you both cut down passing lanes and help provide defensive support and cover for one another. Your position on the field will depend on where your opponent has the ball and if the player on the ball is being pressured. If your mark is more than one pass away from the ball, you can slough off that player (giving that player more room) and help with the overall team defense. If you are an outside player and the ball is on the other side of the field, you can slough off more than if the ball is in the middle of the field. If the opponent is being pressured by your teammate, you can slough off even more. The object is to put more people in the passing lanes and in a smaller space. This makes it more difficult for your opponent to exploit your defense.

You also need to work on your team's depth. If you have all 10 field players in a 30-yard area from end to end, the area to cover is much less than if your defense stretches 50 yards on the field. To keep your opponents in that limited space, backs need to push up as a unit. Once again, the key to a team pushing up and compacting the defense is pressure on the ball. If the offensive player doesn't have time to look up and find a player making a run due to defensive pressure, your team can be compact and difficult to break down.

Always use this rule of thumb: If your potential mark is more than a pass away from getting the ball, you can move away from that mark. Distance increases when it will take more than two passes for your mark to get the ball. Great team defense wins many, many games.

EXCUSES ARE LIKE LOSSES.
EVERYONE HAS THEM EXCEPT CHAMPIONS.

—ALEX MORGAN

Setting the Wall
On a Direct Free Kick: Part 1

Defense

When the defense commits a foul outside the penalty area (18-yard box), many times there is a need for a wall. Sometimes, the goalkeeper will set the wall, while other times a field player will. Remember: The kick could be a direct free kick or an indirect free kick *(see Figure 3.3)*.

A wall is made up of defending players who are supposed to be 10 yards from the ball. Since nobody is allowed to defend the shooter, the wall is there to help protect the goal. Walls are set to protect the near post, leaving the rest of the goal for the goalkeeper to protect. Talented players can still attack the near post with a ball that goes over the wall and under the crossbar on the near-post side of the goal, or a swerved ball that goes around the wall to the near post. It is good to know if the team you are playing has a player that can attack the goal over or

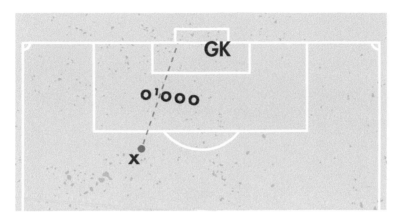

Figure 3.3

around the wall. Your team can then adjust the placement of the wall to help protect against this kind of attack.

When setting the wall, the goalkeeper needs to let their teammates know how many players should be in the wall. The distance of the free kick and the talent level of the player taking it will determine how many players are needed. The better the chance that an offensive player can score, the more players should be in the wall. The offense can play the ball as soon as possible (unless they ask for the referee to move the wall back away from the ball by 10 yards). The free kick cannot be taken until the referee blows the whistle that the ball can be played.

> As a player, know the rules—and use them to your advantage. Learn what fouls result in a direct free kick and what fouls result in an indirect free kick. Rule books are easy to find, and reading them can help your game.

Setting the Wall
On a Direct Free Kick: Part 2

Defense

During a free kick, if the ball is live (the offensive team has not asked the ref to move the wall back to 10 yards from the ball), then one of your teammates should set the wall and the goalkeeper should be alert for a quick kick by the opponents. If the goalkeeper is setting the wall, then the far post is open and the other team can shoot or even pass the ball into the goal. Because of this, it's not a bad idea to have a field player set the wall—usually one of the strikers.

To set the wall, the field player needs to be in a straight line from the near post, through the ball, to the player setting the wall. That player then places a teammate on the end of the wall so that the wall protects the near post. If you are doing this, you should make sure that the player's inside ear is in alignment with the near post. After setting the first player, the rest of the wall lines up beside the end of the wall player. When setting the wall, the field player should point with their arms to eliminate confusion.

While the wall is being set, the goalkeeper needs to survey the field to make sure that players in dangerous positions are marked. Then, the goalkeeper should get in a good position to make a save if the ball is shot directly.

Consider taking a referee course. It will help you understand the nuances of the game. You can also make some money reffing games in your community.

MENTAL
- EXERCISE -

8

It's Your Ball Until Proven Otherwise

General

Many times in a game, a loose ball will just sit there because no one is taking the initiative to get it. As a player, you may think that a teammate is going to get it or that you are leaving your mark open by going to the ball. Remember: The ball is the most important object on the field. Your marks can't get the ball if their team doesn't have possession of it. A loose ball near you is yours until it isn't. Get into the habit of thinking that way.

A couple of things help with this. Throughout the game, have a general picture of where all the other players are positioned and try to anticipate where the ball might go. Of course, when you go after the ball, go hard to win that loose ball. Too many times, you might hesitate and get there too late. That hesitation is usually caused by looking to see who else might get the ball. Tell yourself, "That ball is mine!" immediately. Go after it at pace while looking to see whether a teammate or your opponent will get there first. It is always better to back off after realizing you won't get the ball than to not be aggressive enough in the first place.

This "that ball is mine" attitude can carry over into your tryouts and training. Many players stay in the background and don't step up when a coach asks for volunteers for a drill. Their mind-set might be that they aren't very good at that drill or skill. Generally, coaches like players to take initiative—to put themselves out there to work on their game. It shows that you have a risk-taking attitude—that you're ready for anything. Don't be the shrinking violet.

> Coaches would rather have you make aggressive mistakes than passive mistakes. It is easier for a coach to make an overly aggressive player tone it down than to make a passive player be more aggressive. Always be ready to make things happen.

Move on Corners

Scoring

When your team has a corner and you are trying to score, it is important to make yourself tough to defend. Defending on corners is done three ways: man-to-man defense, zone, or some hybrid combination of zone and man-to-man. No matter what corner defense your opponent is playing, it is critical that you move to make yourself hard to defend.

As a team, your coach should let you know where players need to be to finish the corners. Popular places are the near post, far post, just in front of the goalkeeper, the penalty spot, and around the penalty arc in case balls ricochet. Players need to know where everyone is going and then time runs to get to their designated spot as the ball might arrive. If you arrive early, you are easier to defend.

When the ball arrives, play it aggressively. Try to get a piece of the ball toward goal or in front of goal. If the ball doesn't come to you, adjust your position so that you're ball side—in the best position to score. Balls bouncing around the penalty area in front of the goal cause confusion—and confusion is to the advantage of the offense. Take advantage of it.

If you are being played man-to-man, try to make blind-sided runs so that your marker can't see both you and the ball at the same time. If your destination run ends at a defensive player playing zone, try to arrive at the position as the ball gets there and get to a ball-side position.

When making runs on corners, try to bend your runs so that you are in the path of the incoming ball. If the corner kick is taken early, this positioning will allow you to see it and be in the ball's path.

WHEN PEOPLE TELL YOU, "NO," JUST SMILE
AND TELL THEM, "YES, I CAN."

—JULIE FOUDY

Make Your Weak Foot Acceptable

General

To become the best you can be, you need an array of skills—
and the ability to exercise those skills with both feet. If you are
right footed, your left foot needs to be more than something to
stand on. While many coaches want players to be equally adept
with both feet, a more realistic approach is encapsulated in the
saying, "Make your weak foot acceptable and make your strong
foot lethal."

For example, take Diego Maradona. Maradona could do so
many things with his left foot that he was almost unstoppable.
His right-foot play, though, was just adequate for the high
level where he competed. You are good with your strong foot
because it feels more natural to use it. It is easier to try new
moves, passes, shots, etc., using your strong foot, so make it as
good as it can be.

Still, you need to bring your weaker foot to a level where it
can still contribute on the field. If you can't make an acceptable
pass with your weak foot, your defender will sense that and

force you to that weaker side. Many players have trouble improving a weakness in the midst of the season. In game situations, it feels more comfortable to do what you have always done with your strong foot (even though it might be more effective, positionwise, to use your weak foot). It is better to work on your weak foot during a time where there are no games (or games that don't matter as much).

Practice makes perfect. Now, go out and practice what will make you a more productive player!

After a match, think about what would have made you a better player that day—and practice it. It could be making a move or a shot with your weak foot acceptable or a move with your strong foot that makes you lethal on the pitch.

Get Soccer Strong

Physical

Physically, soccer is a combination of stamina and strength. There are a lot of collisions and a lot of running. While you do not need to be a powerlifter to be a good soccer player (in fact, being a powerlifter would limit your stamina), you do need to get physically strong to withstand the pressures of training and matches. One thing to understand is that you should only measure yourself against yourself. You have a soccer strength potential, and you want to get as close to that individual strength potential as possible—the best that you can be. Strengthwise, you need to work on three basic areas: your legs, your upper body, and your core.

Your lower-body strength is used for striking a ball harder, moving quickly over short distances, and winning one-on-one battles. You want to be strong but not bulky. Soccer players can run up to eight miles in a 90-minute game. Doing that with bulky muscles is nearly impossible. Higher numbers of reps with lighter weight will get you where you need to go in terms of your lower-body stamina and strength.

Your upper body will be used to withstand opponents trying to take the ball from you in tight situations. It will also be used to hold off players running shoulder-to-shoulder down the field when you have the ball. As with your lower body, you want to make your shoulders and arms strong without bulking up. Doing higher number of repetitions with lighter weight (or just your body weight) will help develop your upper-body strength.

Your core is aptly named—it is the center of your soccer development. A strong core will help you put yourself into the many positions that arise during a match. Abdominal work can be done each day—and much can be done just using your body weight (planks, crunches, sit-ups, etc.). Set a routine for daily core work, and you will be a better soccer athlete.

I have a saying: "If you have a chance to play, you should play!" Getting physically strong is important, but nothing makes you a better player than touching the ball. Adding physical training can enhance your game, but perfecting the skills of the game is the most important thing you can do.

MENTAL
EXERCISE
12

Get Game Fit

Physical

As you prepare for an upcoming season, it is important to be in shape for the first training sessions. It is not the coach's responsibility to get you in shape; it is your responsibility. If you are not fit then you won't be able to do your best during training, possibly hurting your chances of making the starting 11—or making the team at all. So how do you get fit?

Too many players simply run to get ready for a season. While running can be good, it is how you run that makes the difference. If you always jog at the same speed, then you will be ready to jog at the same speed on the pitch. During a game, you stand, you walk, you jog, you run, and you sprint. All of this means that you need to do more than aerobic running—you need to do what you'll do during a match. You need to run in both anaerobic and aerobic modes. To do this, you should do fartleks—essentially mix jogging, running, walking, and sprints in your overall program of distance. If you are running on a track, you can employ each of the components at the same place on every lap. If you are running on the road or on trails, pick a light pole or a tree to start and stop each component. As you get fitter, you can lengthen your sprints (the anaerobic part of your workout) and shorten the recovery time between them. You are now running to train for the game.

Training for the game comes into play when training by yourself, with friends, or with the ball. Challenge yourself to develop skills with the ball at speed, and do as many sets as you can in a short period of time. If you are training and the ball gets away during shooting or some other exercise, incorporate a hard run to retrieve it. Remember: When you are tired on the field, your ability level drops. Train accordingly.

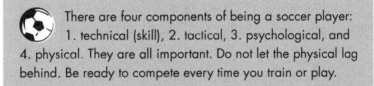

There are four components of being a soccer player: 1. technical (skill), 2. tactical, 3. psychological, and 4. physical. They are all important. Do not let the physical lag behind. Be ready to compete every time you train or play.

Win the Ball: Start the Offense

Defense

When playing defense, it is important to see the whole field and not be zoomed in on only your mark. If the player you are guarding is more than one pass away from getting the ball, your cover position allows you to help your team if someone gets beat or the opposition makes a great through pass, breaking down your team's defense. Even when your mark is only one pass removed from the ball, you should know where your teammates are, as well as your opponents. Having a global picture of where everyone is on the field will help your play.

While on offense, good teams want to spread the field and stretch both deep and wide. At the same time, good teams want to be compact on defense. When you win the ball, you have a great opportunity to break down your opponents' defense—because they're still spread out in offensive mode. It is generally true that teams transition from defense to offense faster than from offense to defense. When winning the ball, always look for ways to exploit the transitioning defensive team by making a one-touch pass to a player further up the field, dribbling forward to space, or making a quick penetrating cross to change the point of attack and put the opposition on their heels.

Your mind-set should be to do more than just win the ball. You should be ready to start the offense quickly. To do this, it helps to have an overview of the field and the confidence that you can win the ball and immediately start the offense. The quicker you attack on these counter opportunities, the more successful you will be.

> During drills, make it a point to win the ball and play it quickly. The more you do this, the more confident you will become and the more adept you will be at winning the ball and playing it quickly during a match.

MENTAL
– EXERCISE –

14

Working the Ball Out of the Back

Possession

When a team wants to keep position, they start by working the ball out of the back. Too many times, players think that working it out of the back only involves the goalkeeper and the defenders. But working it out of the back is really an 11-person activity—one that begins with the backs and the goalkeeper. The backs do need to spread the field. Many times, they will take the shape of an umbrella with the top of the umbrella pointing toward their own goal. Since all systems in soccer have more defenders than the opponent has strikers, the initial part of working out of the back has the four defenders (maybe three) and the goalkeeper going against one, two, or three strikers. This numerical advantage should allow your team to keep the ball. Of course, the farther up the field you go with the ball, the more that numerical advantage shifts.

The back five (including the goalkeeper) need to pass the ball to one another while looking for a penetrating pass to a

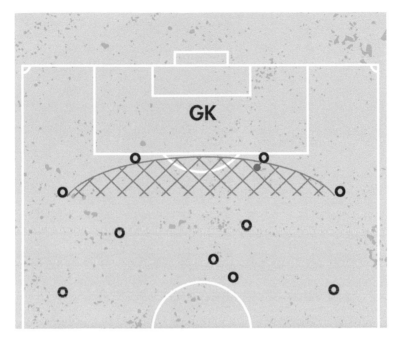

Figure 3.4

midfielder checking to the ball. Many times, that midfielder will be marked and will pass the ball back to the defenders. As a defender, you are trying to probe the opponent's defense and keep moving them out of position so your midfielder can have time and space to turn and face the opponent's goal. The more accurate passes you can make while moving up the field, the more likely you are to soften up the defense and make them chase the ball. To get a better numerical advantage, many teams will have their outside backs move up the field to help with possession in the middle third of the field. This gives your team a numerical advantage in the midfield. Of course, you must be vigilant, since your team will only have the two center backs and the goalkeeper back *(see Figure 3.4)*.

From the middle third, probe and find passes to players in the final third (offensive third of the field) to attack the goal. Once there, midfielders (and maybe even the outside backs) can attack the goal.

> Working it out of the back cannot be achieved without great and consistent technique with the ball. Having all 11 players on your team with this technique can pay benefits at the end of the game in terms of fatigue.

I GENUINELY WANT TO DO MY BEST EVERY DAY, AND I GENUINELY WANT TO ENJOY LIFE EVERY DAY.

—LANDON DONOVAN

Beating the Offside Trap

Scoring

An offside trap happens when a team steps forward as a group (usually the back four defenders) to make one or more players on your team offside. Many times, the strikers end up offside because they don't adjust their position when the defense steps up. And even if your strikers do adjust, they are no longer in a position to get a through ball because they are moving in the wrong direction *(see Figure 3.5)*.

Since the offside trap mainly tries to trap the strikers, to beat the trap, your team needs forward runs from players other than the strikers. If you are a midfielder, you should anticipate the trap and start moving forward as the trap moves forward. Your teammate with the ball can now slot the ball in the gaps of the defenders, allowing you a one-on-one with the goalkeeper. You should also have time to beat the goalkeeper since the defenders were heading away from goal as you were heading toward it. Take your time and finish the opportunity.

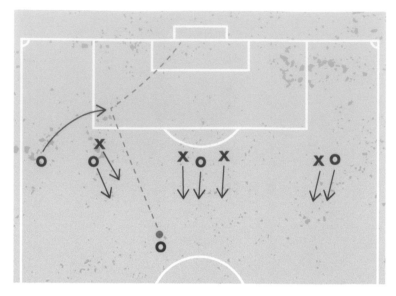

Figure 3.5

Another way to beat the offside trap is by dribbling. A good offside trap is accompanied by pressure on the ball. However, if you have the ball and can beat your defender, you can push the ball forward, split the defenders, and go to the goal.

Timing by the entire team is very important. The strikers need to adjust to stay in an onside position. Midfielders need to time runs so that they are onside when the ball is played. They must also go to a space where a teammate can find them on a pass. If you are dribbling to beat the trap, time your big touch through the defenders when they are focused on pulling your teammates offside.

> A team utilizing an offside trap is there to be beaten. In almost all cases, playing solid basic team defense is a better alternative to the trap.

GLOSSARY

aerobic: An exercise that uses available oxygen to maximum use (example: jogging)

anaerobic: An exercise that puts a person in oxygen debt, forcing use of oxygen in the body (example: multiple sprints)

ask for 10: When a player asks the referee to move the wall to 10 yards from the ball

ball side: When a player is closer to the ball than an opponent

beat behind: The object of an offensive player—to get by the defender closer to the offensive player's goal

beating touch: The final part of beating a player off the dribble by getting behind the defender

blind-sided run: A player without the ball runs behind a defender so that the defender can't see the ball and the player at the same time

both sides of the ball: Playing both offense and defense

box to box: Refers to playing the whole field, from penalty area to penalty area

broken-down position: A position where the defensive player is in a low position on the balls of the feet when guarding a player with the ball

changing the point of attack: When the ball goes from one side of the field to the other

check away: When a player who doesn't have the ball runs away from the player with the ball to open space to come back closer to ball for a pass

check back or check to: When a player moves toward their teammate to receive the ball

close you down: When a defender gets closer to the offensive player who is receiving the ball

distribution: When the goalkeeper begins the play with a throw, a roll, a punt, or a goal kick

dives in: When a defensive player sticks a foot in to try to steal the ball

dead balls: Balls that restart the game on the field with corner kicks, goal kicks, free kicks, or throw-ins

early cross: When an offensive player crosses the ball toward goal from 20 or more yards from goal

fartlek: A running regimen that uses a combination of walking, jogging, running, and sprinting

4-3-3: A common formation made up of four backs, three midfielders, and three forwards

50/50 balls: A free-ball situation where both players have an equal chance of playing the ball

lead foot: The foot closer to the goal when a player is passing to a teammate

lock your ankle: Putting your toe down (instep shot) or up (inside of the foot pass) to make your foot a solid striking area

numerical advantage or numerical superiority: When a team has more players in an area than their opponent

man on: When a defender is marking an offensive player; a call by a teammate to let a player who is about to receive the ball know that a defender is in a good defending position

offside trap: When a team tries to pull a team offside by stepping up as a group in front of the strikers just before the ball is passed

off your line: When a goalkeeper comes off the goal line to cut down angles and play the ball offensively

open space: An area where there are no players

parry: When a goalkeeper pushes a ball with the hands to make a save; many times done when the goalkeeper can't catch the ball

pushing up: When a team moves up the field—usually when the backs move up when teammates have the ball farther up the field

quick restart: After a foul is called, putting the ball in play quickly to catch the defense off guard

run of play: When the ball is in play; the opposite of a dead ball

side volley: A shot that is taken from the side of the body, usually when the ball is off the ground

spin turn: When a dribbling player uses the body to keep a defender away from the ball and turns to open space

square pass: A pass to a teammate that is at a 90-degree angle from the ball

strength potential: The ultimate ability of an individual in terms of becoming stronger

take the goalkeeper out of play: When crossing the ball, placing the ball where the goalkeeper can't safely get to it in the air

wall: A defensive setup to protect the goal on a potential goal-scoring free kick

working the ball out of the back: When a team works the ball up the field with passing, starting with the goalkeeper and the backs

RESOURCES

Watching highlights of various professional league matches can show you the skills and small-sided tactics of this beautiful game. Below are some links to the English Premier League, LaLiga (Spain), the Union of European Football Associations Champions League, and the three U.S. domestic leagues: Major League Soccer, National Women's Soccer League, and the United Soccer League.

- ▶ https://www.premierleague.com/video
- ▶ https://www.youtube.com/user/mls
- ▶ https://www.youtube.com/channel/UCNyM7kXK2ML unZtStlc-atg
- ▶ http://www.uefa.com/uefachampionsleague/video/ highlights
- ▶ https://www.uslsoccer.com/highlights
- ▶ http://www.nwslsoccer.com/videos

To get a sense of the game as a whole, it is great to watch full games either live on TV or streaming online. There are many outlets to watch the world's top leagues, the U.S. domestic leagues, and American collegiate games, as most put their games online. Watching full games will give you a feel for the flow of the game and the various set plays that occur. As a student of the game, you should concentrate on how the set plays are handled by teams on the offense and defense.

If you want to improve your ball skills, look into a concentrated skill format called the Coerver method. Make sure that you force yourself to practice at speed to the point of failure (and past). By doing this, your skills will hold up in the speed of game conditions.

▶ http://www.coerver.co.uk/shop/c/23/dvds-books

Finally, a good book to read about how your determination can help you surpass players who have more presumed talent than you is *Grit: The Power of Passion and Perseverance* by Angela Duckworth.

INDEX

ABOUT THE AUTHOR

Charlie Slagle is the Chief Executive Officer of the Tampa Bay United Soccer Club. Previously he was the Executive Director of the Colorado Rapids Youth Soccer Club in Denver CO, and the CEO of the Capital Area Soccer League in Raleigh NC. He coached the men's soccer team at Davidson College for 21 seasons, and he was the NCAA Division I coach of the Year in 1992, the Southern Regional Coach of the Year in 1990 and 1992, and the Southern Conference Coach of the Year seven times. Slagle is a past president of the National Soccer Coaches Association of America and a member of the NC Soccer Hall of Fame and the Davidson College Athletics Hall of Fame.

CPSIA information can be obtained
at www.ICGtesting.com
Printed in the USA
LVHW01s1722260918
591423LV00003B/3/P